Table of Contents

Table of Contents

Name: _____

Spelling: Short Vowels

Vowels are the letters **a, e, i, o, u** and sometimes **y**. There are five short vowels: **ă** as in **a**pple, **ĕ** as in **e**gg and br**ea**th, **ĭ** as in s**i**ck, **ŏ** as in t**o**p and **ŭ** as in **u**p.

Directions: Complete the exercises using words from the box.

blend	insist	health	pump	crop
fact	pinch	pond	hatch	plug

1. Write each word under its vowel sound.

   ă   ĕ   ĭ   ŏ   ŭ

   _____ _____ _____ _____ _____

   _____ _____ _____ _____ _____

2. Complete these sentences, using a word with the vowel sound given. Use each word from the box only once.

   Here's an interesting (ă) _____ about your (ĕ) _____.

   Henry was very pleased with his corn (ŏ) _____.

   The boys enjoyed fishing in the (ŏ) _____.

   They (ĭ) _____ on watching the egg (ă) _____.

   (ĕ) _____ in a (ĭ) _____ of salt.

   The farmer had to (ŭ) _____ water from the lake for his cows to drink.

   Did you put the (ŭ) _____ in the bathtub this time?

Name: _____

Spelling: Short Vowels

Directions: Read the words. After each, write the correct vowel sound. Underline the letter or letters that spell the sound in the word. The first one has been done for you.

Word	Vowel		Word	Vowel
1. str<u>u</u>ck	U	9. breath	____
2. scramble	____	10. edge	____
3. strong	____	11. kick	____
4. chill	____	12. stop	____
5. thud	____	13. quiz	____
6. dread	____	14. brush	____
7. plunge	____	15. crash	____
8. mask	____	16. dodge	____

Directions: List four words (nouns and verbs) with short vowel sounds. Then write two sentences using the words.

Example: Ann, can, hand, Pam
Ann can give Pam a hand.

_____

_____

_____

_____

1. _____

_____

2. _____

_____

Name: _____

Writing: Sentences

A **sentence** is a group of words that expresses a complete thought.

Directions: Write **S** by each group of words that is a sentence and **NS** by those that are not a complete sentence.

Examples:

<u>NS</u> A pinch of salt in the soup.

<u>S</u> Grandmother was fond of her flower garden.

_____ 1. Tigers blend in with their surroundings.

_____ 2. Our crop of vegetables for this summer.

_____ 3. Don't forget to put the plug in the sink.

_____ 4. Usually older people in good health.

_____ 5. Fond of lying in the sun for hours.

_____ 6. Will ducks hatch a swan egg?

_____ 7. I hope he won't insist on coming with us.

_____ 8. Regular exercise will pump up your muscles.

_____ 9. A fact printed in all the newspapers.

_____10. Did you pinch the baby?

_____11. Plug the hole with your finger.

_____12. A new teacher today in health class.

_____13. I insist on giving you some of my candy.

_____14. A blend of peanut butter and honey.

_____15. As many facts as possible in your report.

5

© 2001 McGraw Hill.

Sentences: Subjects

The **subject** of a sentence tells you who or what the sentence is about. A subject is either a common or proper noun.

Examples: Sue went to the store.

Sue is the subject of the sentence.

The tired boys and girls walked home slowly.

The tired boys and girls is the subject of the sentence.

Directions: Underline the subject of each sentence.
The first one has been done for you.

1. The birthday cake was pink and white.
2. Anthony celebrated his fourth birthday.
3. The tower of building blocks fell over.
4. On Saturday, our family will go to a movie.
5. The busy editor was writing sentences.
6. Seven children painted pictures.
7. Two happy dolphins played cheerfully on the surf.
8. A sand crab buried itself in the dunes.
9. Blue waves ran peacefully ashore.
10. Sleepily, she went to bed.

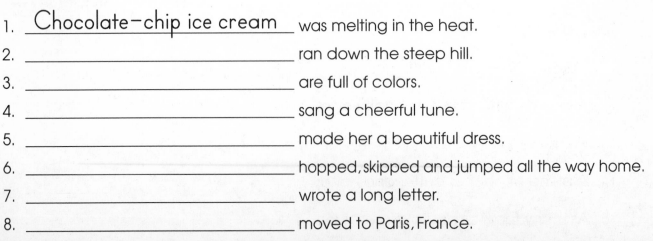

Directions: Write a subject for each sentence.

1. Chocolate-chip ice cream _____ was melting in the heat.
2. _____ ran down the steep hill.
3. _____ are full of colors.
4. _____ sang a cheerful tune.
5. _____ made her a beautiful dress.
6. _____ hopped, skipped and jumped all the way home.
7. _____ wrote a long letter.
8. _____ moved to Paris, France.

Sentences: Predicates

The **predicate** of a sentence tells what the subject is doing. The predicate contains the action, linking and/or helping verb.

Examples: Sue went to the store.

> **Went to the store** is the predicate.

> The tired boys and girls walked home slowly.

> **Walked home slowly** is the predicate.

Hint: When identifying the predicate, look for the verb. The verb is usually the first word of the predicate.

Directions: Underline the predicate in each sentence with two lines. The first one has been done for you.

1. The choir sang joyfully.
2. Their song had both high and low notes.
3. Sal played the piano while they sang.
4. This Sunday the orchestra will have a concert in the park.
5. John is working hard on his homework.
6. He will write a report on electricity.
7. The report will tell about Ben Franklin's kite experiment.
8. Jackie, Mary and Amy played on the swings.
9. They also climbed the rope ladder.
10. Before the girls went home, they slid down the slide.

Directions: Write a predicate for each sentence.

1. Sam and Libby _ran to school_.
2. At school, the children _were ~~the~~ late_.
3. The football team _stunk_.
4. Seven silly serpents _X_.
5. At the zoo, the animals _escaped_.

Name: _____

Writing: Subjects and Predicates

Directions: Draw a line to connect the subjects with the correct predicates to make complete sentences.

Subjects

1. The busy mall
2. The restaurants
3. The children
4. Mom
5. The baby

Predicates

went to sleep in her stroller.

bought two new dresses.

was full of shoppers.

served delicious food.

purchased new sneakers for school.

SUBJECT & PREDICATE

Directions: Read the following sentences. Underline the subject once and the predicate twice. The first one has been done for you.

1. The busy editor wrote a page about subjects and predicates.

2. She was hopeful the children would understand sentences.

3. The school children completed their pages quickly.

4. When their work was finished, they went outside.

5. The teacher watched the boys play ball.

6. The girls swung on the swings and climbed the monkey bars.

7. Kim, Luke, Jill and Matt enjoyed their time outdoors.

8. They were refreshed when they came inside.

9. The children ran outside after the storm.

10. Fall had always been her favorite time of year.

Name: _____

Spelling: Listening for Vowels

Directions: Circle the word in each row with the same vowel sound as the first word. The first one has been done for you.

blend	twig	brand	(fed)	bleed
fact	first	bad	shell	bead
plug	card	steal	stuff	plan
pinch	kiss	reach	ripe	come
health	dear	bath	top	head
crop	hope	stock	drip	strap

Directions: Write the words from the box that answer the questions.

blend	insist	health	pump	crop	fact	pinch	fond	hatch	plug

1. Which two words have the same vowel as the first vowel in **bundle**?

   _____ , _____

2. Which two words have the same vowel as the first vowel in **bottle**?

   _____ , _____

3. Which two words have the same vowel as the first vowel in **wilderness**?

   _____ , _____

4. Which two words have the same vowel as the first vowel in **manner**?

   _____ , _____

5. Which two words have the same vowel as the first vowel in **measure**?

   _____ , _____

Name: _____

Kinds of Sentences: Statements and Questions

A **statement** tells some kind of information. It is followed by a period (.).

Examples: It is a rainy day. We are going to the beach next summer.

A **question** asks for a specific piece of information. It is followed by a question mark (?).

Examples: What is the weather like today? When are you going to the beach?

Directions: Write whether each sentence is a statement or question. The first one has been done for you.

1. Jamie went for a walk at the zoo. _____statement_____

2. The leaves turn bright colors in the fall. _____

3. When does the Easter Bunny arrive? _____

4. Madeleine went to the new art school. _____

5. Is school over at 3:30? _____

6. Grandma and Grandpa are moving. _____

7. Anthony went home. _____

8. Did Mary go to Amy's house? _____

9. Who went to work late? _____

10. Ms. McDaniel is a good teacher. _____

Directions: Write two statements and two questions below.

Statements:

_____

_____

Questions:

_____

_____

Kinds of Sentences: Commands and Exclamations

A **command** tells someone to do something. It is followed by a period (.).

Examples: Get your math book. Do your homework.

An **exclamation** shows strong feeling or excitement.
It is followed by an exclamation mark (!).

Examples: Watch out for that car! Oh, no! There's a snake!

Directions: Write whether each sentence is a command or exclamation. The first one has been done for you.

1. Please clean your room. _____command_____

2. Wow! Those fireworks are beautiful! _____exclamation_____

3. Come to dinner now. _____

4. Color the sky and water blue. _____

5. Trim the paper carefully. _____

6. Hurry, here comes the bus! _____

7. Isn't that a lovely picture! _____

8. Time to stop playing and clean up. _____

9. Brush your teeth before bedtime. _____

10. Wash your hands before you eat! _____

Directions: Write two commands and two exclamations below.

Commands:

_____

_____

Exclamations:

_____

_____

Name: _____

Writing: Four Kinds of Sentences

Directions: Write **S** for statement, **Q** for question, **C** for command or **E** for exclamation. End each sentence with a period, question mark or exclamation mark.

Example: __E__ You better watch out!

_____ 1. My little brother insists on coming with us

_____ 2. Tell him movies are bad for his health

_____ 3. He says he's fond of movies

_____ 4. Does he know there are monsters in this movie

_____ 5. He says he needs facts for his science report

_____ 6. He's writing about something that hatched from an old egg

_____ 7. Couldn't he just go to the library

_____ 8. Could we dress him like us so he'll blend in

_____ 9. Are you kidding

_____ 10. Would he sit by himself at the movie

_____ 11. That would be too dangerous

_____ 12. Mom said she'd give us money for candy if we took him with us

_____ 13. Why didn't you say that earlier

_____ 14. Get your brother and let's go

Name:_____

Spelling: Making New Words

Directions: Use words from the box to answer the questions.

blend	fond
fact	pump
insist	hatch
pinch	crop
health	plug

1. Change or drop one letter in each word to make a word from the word box.

face _____   plump _____

wealth _____   food _____

blind _____   slug _____

drop _____   watch _____

2. Gradually change **pinch** to a word from the box.

p	**i**	**n**	**c**	**h**
_____	_____	t	_____	_____
_____	a	_____	_____	_____
h	_____	_____	_____	_____

3. Which word begins like **house** and has the same vowel as the first one in **feather**? _____

4. Which word begins like **cake** and has the same vowel as **hot**? _____

5. Which word ends like **hot** and has the same vowel as **strap**? _____

Name: _____

Spelling: Word Ladders

Word ladders are a fun way of creating new words by changing one letter/sound in the original word.

Example:

hat

bat

bet

bed

By changing one letter with each step, the word **hat** is changed to **bed**.

Directions: Change each word below to a new word. Write the first letter of the name of each picture in the blank above the arrow. The first one has been done for you.

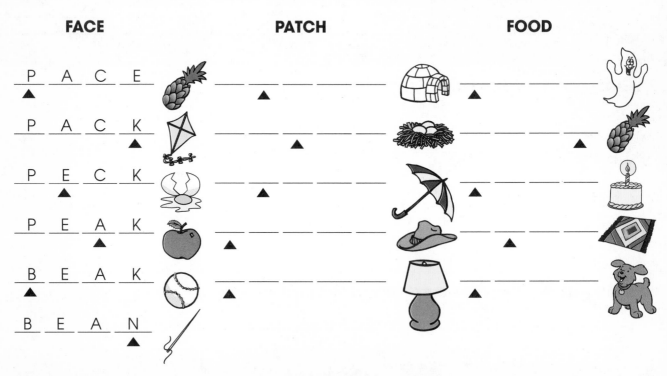

FACE   PATCH   FOOD

P A C E
▲

P A C K
      ▲

P E C K
   ▲

P E A K
   ▲

B E A K
▲

B E A N
      ▲

Make a word ladder of your own. Begin with the word **HEALTH**.

Name:_____

Writing: Four Kinds of Sentences

Directions: For each pair of words, write two kinds of sentences (any combination of question, command, statement or exclamation). Use one or both words in each sentence. Name each kind of sentence you wrote.

Example: pump   crop

Question: <u>What kind of crops did you plant?</u>

Command: <u>Pump the water as fast as you can</u>.

1. pinch   health

_____ : _____

_____ : _____

2. fond   fact

_____ : _____

_____ : _____

3. insist   hatch

_____ : _____

_____ : _____

exclamation   command   statement   question

Name: _____

Writing: Verbs

Verbs are the action words in a sentence. There are three kinds of verbs: action verbs, linking verbs and helping verbs.

An **action verb** tells the action of a sentence.

Examples: run, hop, skip, sleep, jump, talk, snore
Michael **ran** to the store. **Ran** is the action verb.

A **linking verb** joins the subject and predicate of a sentence.

Examples: am, is, are, was, were
Michael **was** at the store. **Was** is the linking verb.

A **helping verb** is used with an action verb to "help" the action of the sentence.

Examples: am, is, are, was, were
Matthew **was** helping Michael. **Was** helps the action verb **helping**.

Directions: Read the following sentences. Underline the verbs. Above each, write **A** for action verb, **L** for linking verb and **H** for helping verb. The first one has been done for you.

     A
1. Amy <u>jumps</u> rope.

2. Paul was jumping rope, too.

3. They were working on their homework.

4. The math problem requires a lot of thinking.

5. Addition problems are fun to do.

6. The baby sleeps in the afternoon.

7. Grandma is napping also.

8. Sam is going to bed.

9. John paints a lovely picture of the sea.

10. The colors in the picture are soft and pale.

Writing: Verb Tense

Not only do verbs tell the action of a sentence but they also tell when the action takes place. This is called the **verb tense**. There are three verb tenses: past, present and future tense.

Present-tense verbs tell what is happening now.

Example: Jane **spells** words with long vowel sounds.

Past-tense verbs tell about action that has already happened. Past-tense verbs are usually formed by adding **ed** to the verb.

Example: stay — stayed
John **stayed** home yesterday.

Past-tense verbs can also be made by adding helping verbs **was** or **were** before the verb and adding **ing** to the verb.

Example: talk — was talking
Sally **was talking** to her mom.

Future-tense verbs tell what will happen in the future. Future-tense verbs are made by putting the word **will** before the verb.

Example: paint — will paint
Susie and Sherry **will paint** the house.

Directions: Read the following verbs. Write whether the verb tense is past, present or future.

Verb	Tense	Verb	Tense
1. watches	present	8. writes	_____
2. wanted	_____	9. vaulted	_____
3. will eat	_____	10. were sleeping	_____
4. was squawking	_____	11. will sing	_____
5. yawns	_____	12. is speaking	_____
6. crawled	_____	13. will cook	_____
7. will hunt	_____	14. likes	_____

Name: _____

Writing: Verb Tense

Directions: Read the following sentences. Underline the verbs. Above each verb, write whether it is past, present or future tense.

        past

1. The crowd <u>was booing</u> the referee.

2. Sally will compete on the balance beam.

3. Matt marches with the band.

4. Nick is marching, too.

5. The geese swooped down to the pond.

6. Dad will fly home tomorrow.

7. They were looking for a new book.

8. Presently, they are going to the garden.

9. The children will pick the ripe vegetables.

10. Grandmother canned the green beans.

Directions: Write six sentences of your own using the correct verb tense.

Past tense:

_____

_____

Present tense:

_____

_____

Future tense:

_____

_____

Writing: Present-Tense Verbs

Directions: Write two sentences for each verb below. Tell about something that is happening now and write the verb as both simple present tense and present tense with a helping verb.

Example: run

Mia runs to the store.   Mia is running to the store.

1. hatch

_____

_____

2. check

_____

_____

3. spell

_____

_____

4. blend

_____

_____

5. lick

_____

_____

6. cry

_____

_____

7. write

_____

_____

8. dream

_____

_____

Name: _____

Review

Directions: Read the sentence below. Circle all five short vowels. (Two words in the sentence do not have short vowels.)

P a t   b e n t   t o   p i c k   u p   t h e   d o g.

Directions: Pretend you are going to meet the president of the United States or the prime minister of Canada. Write the sentences below. Make sure they are complete thoughts and end with a period, question mark or exclamation mark.

1. Write a question you would ask.

   _____

   _____

2. Write a statement you would make: one thing you think this person should know about you or about the country. For this sentence, use **is** or **are** and add **ing** to the verbs.

   _____

   _____

3. Write a command: one thing you would like this person to do. (Remember to say "please.")

   _____

   _____

4. Write one exclamation that shows how you feel about meeting him/her.

   _____

   _____

Name: _____

Spelling: Long e and a

Long **ē** can be spelled **ea** as in **real** or **ee** as in **deer**. Long **ā** can be spelled **a** as in **apron**, **ai** as in **pail**, **ay** as in **pay** or **a-e** as in **lake**.

Directions: Complete the exercises with words from the box.

deal	clay	grade	weave	stream
pain	tape	sneeze	claim	treat

1. Write each word in the row with the matching vowel sound.

    ā _____ _____ _____ _____ _____

    ē _____ _____ _____ _____ _____

2. Complete each sentence, using a word with the vowel sound given. Use each word from the word box only once.

    Everyone in (**ā**) _____ four ate an ice-cream (**ē**) _____.

    Every time I (**ē**) _____, I feel (**ā**) _____ in my chest.

    When I (**ē**) _____ with yarn, I put a piece of (**ā**) _____ on the loose ends so they won't come undone.

    You (**ā**) _____ you got a good (**ē**) _____ on your new bike, but I still think you paid too much.

    We camped beside a (**ē**) _____.

    We forgot to wrap up our (**ā**) _____ and it dried out.

Name: _____

Spelling: Long e and a

When a vowel is long, it sounds the same as its letter name.

Examples: Long ē as in **treat**, **eel**, **complete**.
Long ā as in **ape**, **trail**, **say**, **apron**.

Directions: Read the words. After each word, write the correct vowel sound. Underline the letter or letters that spell the sound in the word. The first one has been done for you.

Word	Vowel		Word	Vowel
1. sp<u>ee</u>ch	e	9. plate	
2. grain		10. breeze	
3. deal		11. whale	
4. baste		12. clay	
5. teach		13. veal	
6. waiting		14. apron	
7. cleaning		15. raining	
8. crane		16. freezer	

Directions: Choose one long vowel sound. On another sheet of paper, list six words (nouns and verbs) that have that sound. Below, write two sentences using the words.

Example: freeze, teaches, breeze, speech, keep, Eve

Eve teaches speech in the breeze.

_____

_____

Name: _____

Spelling: Vowel Sounds

Directions: Follow the instructions below.

1. Circle the word in each row with the same vowel sound as the first word. The first one has been done for you.

deal	pail	church	(greet)	stove
pain	free	frame	twice	whole
weave	grape	stripe	least	thrill
grade	teach	case	joke	leave
treat	greed	throw	tent	truck

2. Write a word from the box that rhymes with each word below.

deal	clay	grade	weave	stream	pain	tape	sneeze	claim	treat

lame _____

may _____

cream _____

laid _____

feet _____

shape _____

feel _____

leave _____

drain _____

trees _____

3. The words below are written the way they are pronounced. Write the word from the box that sounds like:

klā _____

wēv _____

dēl _____

strēm _____

tāp _____

klām _____

trēt _____

grād _____

pān _____

snēz _____

Name: _____

Writing: Nouns

A **noun** names a person, place or thing.

Examples: **Persons** — boy, girl, Mom, Dad
Places — park, pool, house, office
Things — bike, swing, desk, book

Directions: Read the following sentences.
Underline the nouns. The first one has been done for you.

1. The girl went to school.

2. Grandma and Grandpa will visit us soon.

3. The bike is in the garage.

4. Dad went to his office.

5. Mom is at her desk in the den.

6. John's house is near the park.

7. Her brothers are at school.

8. We took the books to the library.

Directions: Read the following words. Underline the nouns. Then categorize the nouns on another sheet of paper into groups of people, places and things.

tree	Mrs. Smith	Dad	cards	Grandma	skip	sell
house	car	truck	Mom	office	grass	sign
boy	run	Sam	stove	greet	grade	school
girl	camp	jump	weave	free	driver	room
salesperson	sad	teach	treat	stripe	paint	Jane
clay	man	leave	happy	play	desk	tape
watch	lives	painter	brother	rain	window	hop

Writing: Common and Proper Nouns

Common nouns name general people, places and things.

Examples: boy, girl, cat, dog, park, city, building

Proper nouns name specific persons, places and things.

Examples: John, Mary, Fluffy, Rover, Central Park, Chicago, Empire State Building

Proper nouns begin with capital letters.

Directions: Read the following nouns. On the blanks, indicate whether the nouns are common or proper. The first two have been done for you.

1. New York City   <u>proper</u>
2. house   <u>common</u>
3. car   _____
4. Ohio   _____
5. river   _____
6. Rocky Mountains   _____
7. Mrs. Jones   _____
8. nurse   _____

9. Dr. DiCarlo   _____
10. man   _____
11. Rock River   _____
12. building   _____
13. lawyer   _____
14. Grand Canyon   _____
15. city   _____
16. state   _____

On another sheet of paper, write proper nouns for the above common nouns.

Directions: Read the following sentences. Underline the common nouns. Circle the proper nouns.

1. Mary's birthday is Friday, October 7.
2. She likes having her birthday in a fall month.
3. Her friends will meet her at the Video Arcade for a party.
4. Ms. McCarthy and Mr. Landry will help with the birthday party games.
5. Mary's friends will play video games all afternoon.
6. Amy and John will bring refreshments and games to the party.

Name: _____

Writing: Nouns or Verbs?

Directions: Write one of the words from the box in each sentence pair. Write **N** over the word if it is used as a noun and **V** if it is used as a verb. You may need to add **s**, **es**, **ing** or **ed** to the verbs.

Example: The girl **sneezes**. Her **sneeze** scares the dog.

(V over sneezes, N over sneeze)

sneeze	tape
claim	treat
grade	stream
date	deal

1. I _____ around flowers. My _____ is louder than your

   _____.

2. Let's go buy a _____ at the store. Today, I will _____ you to a candy bar.

3. Sometimes we _____ our own papers. I always get a higher

   _____ than Josh.

4. The rain _____ down the window. The _____ behind our house is overflowing.

5. Please _____ that TV show for me. I will watch the _____ when I come home.

6. A boy in my class _____ I took his candy bar. I know his _____ is wrong.

7. My brother has a _____ tonight. He _____ the girl who lives next door.

8. Please _____ the cards. While we play, I'll tell you about the _____ I made with my sister.

SPELLING 4

Writing: Using Fewer Words

Writing can be more interesting when fewer words are used. Combining sentences is easy when the subjects are the same. Notice how the comma is used.

Example: Sally woke up. Sally ate breakfast. Sally brushed her teeth.

Sally woke up, ate breakfast and brushed her teeth.

Combining sentences with more than one subject is a little more complicated. Notice how commas are used to "set off" information.

Examples: Jane went to the store. Jane is Sally's sister.

Jane went to the store with Sally, her sister.

Eddie likes to play with cars. Eddie is my younger brother.

Eddie, my younger brother, likes to play with cars.

Directions: Write each pair of sentences as one sentence.

1. Jerry played soccer after school. He played with his best friend, Tom.

   _____

2. Spot likes to chase cats. Spot is my dog.

   _____

3. Lori and Janice both love ice cream. Janice is Lori's cousin.

   _____

4. Jayna is my cousin. Jayna helped me move into my new apartment.

   _____

5. Romeo is a big tomcat. Romeo loves to hunt mice.

   _____

Writing: Using Fewer Words

Directions: Write each pair of sentences as one sentence.

Example: After school, Jerry ate some chocolate
ice cream. It's his favorite treat.

Jerry ate his favorite treat, chocolate ice cream, after school.

1. Benny keeps sneezing. Benny is my brother.

   _____

2. Kelly was dealing the cards. Kelly is my cousin.

   _____

3. Chris is in tenth grade. Chris is my baby-sitter.

   _____

4. Anna has a pain in her hand. Anna is my neighbor.

   _____

5. I have two tapes of the Lipsticks. The Lipsticks are my favorite band.

   _____

6. Jenny likes to play in the stream. Jenny is my sister.

   _____

7. Rachel brought me a treat. Rachel is my good friend.

   _____

8. Judy Blume wrote this book. She is a very popular author.

   _____

9. Mr. Thomas gave me this clay. Mr. Thomas is my teacher.

   _____

10. I'm going to weave a rug in blue and white. Those are the colors in my bedroom.

    _____

Name: _____

Writing: Past-Tense Verbs

To write about something that already happened, you can add **ed** to the verb.

Example: Yesterday, we **talked**.

You can also use **was** and **were** and add **ing** to the verb.

Example: Yesterday, we **were talking**.
When a verb ends with **e**, you usually drop the **e** before adding **ing**.

Examples: grade — was grading   weave — were weaving
                tape — was tapingsneeze — were sneezing

Directions: Write two sentences for each verb below. Tell about something that has already happened and write the verb both ways.
(Watch the spelling of the verbs that end with **e**.)

Example: stream

The rain streamed down the window.

The rain was streaming down the window.

1. grade

_____

_____

2. tape

_____

_____

3. weave

_____

_____

4. sneeze

_____

_____

29

Writing: Putting Ideas Together

Directions: Write each pair of sentences as one sentence.

Example: Jim will deal the cards one at a time. Jim will give four cards to everyone.

Jim will deal the cards one at a time and give four cards to everyone.

1. Amy won the contest.   Amy claimed the prize.

_____

2. We need to find the scissors.   We need to buy some tape.

_____

3. The stream runs through the woods.   The stream empties into the East River.

_____

_____

4. Katie tripped on the steps.   Katie has a pain in her left foot.

_____

_____

5. Grandpa took me to the store.   Grandpa bought me a treat.

_____

6. Charity ran 2 miles.   She walked 1 mile to cool down afterwards.

_____

_____

MASTER SKILLS
SPELLING 4

Spelling: Making New Words

Directions: Unscramble these letters to spell the ā and ē words you have been practicing. If you need help with spelling, look at the box on page 23. The first one has been done for you.

ay + lc   = ___clay___

ea + mtrs = _____

ea + vew   = _____

ea + rtt   = _____

ea + ld   = _____

ee + zsne = _____

a-e + pt   = _____

a-e + drg   = _____

ai + np   = _____

ai + mlc   = _____

Directions: Circle the spelling mistakes and write the words correctly. The first one has been done for you.

1. We made statues out of (cley)

2. Do you ever fish in that streem?

3. Jason sneesed really loudly in class.

4. Running gives me a pane in my side.

5. We are tapeing the show for you.

6. She klaims she won, but I came in first.

7. Would you share your treet with me?

8. He is gradeing our papers right now.

9. She is weeving a placemat of ribbons.

10. What is the big deel, anyway?

___clay___

_____

_____

_____

_____

_____

_____

_____

_____

_____

Review

Directions: Circle the letters that spell the two ē vowels and three ā vowels in the sentence below.

Kay needs ice cream to go with her plain cake.

Directions: For the two bold words, write **N** over the noun and **V** over the verb. Combine the sentence pairs. Change each verb to include a helping verb such as **was** or **were** and add **ing**.

Example:

    V   N

My dad **taped** a TV **show**. It was a football game.

My dad was taping a TV show, a football game.

1. John **paddled** down the **stream**. John was our guide.

   _____

2. He **weaved** a placemat. It was a **present** for his grandmother.

   _____

3. Pete **claimed** he won the **game**. Pete is my neighbor.

   _____

4. My sister **treated** us to ice cream. My sister's name is **Polly**.

   _____

5. Maria **sneezed** while we were at the **fair**. Maria is my cousin.

   _____

6. Julie and Kim **pounded** the **clay**. They are my twin sisters.

   _____

7. Bobby **complained** about a **pain** in his foot. Bobby is the pitcher on our team.

   _____

Name: _____

Spelling: Long i and o

Long **ī** can be spelled **i** as in **wild**, **igh** as in **night**, **i-e** as in **wipe** or **y** as in **try**. Long **ō** can be spelled **o** as in **most**, **oa** as in **toast**, **ow** as in **throw** or **o-e** as in **hope**.

| stripe | groan | glow | toast | grind | fry | sight | stove | toads | flight |

Directions: Complete the exercises with words from the box.

1. Write each word from the box with its vowel sound.

ī _____

ō _____

2. Complete these sentences, using a word with the given vowel sound. Use each word from the box only once.

We will (**ī**) _____ potatoes on the (**ō**) _____.

I thought I heard a low (**ō**) _____, but when I looked, there was nothing

in (**ī**) _____.

The airplane for our (**ī**) _____ had a (**ī**) _____ painted on its side.

I saw a strange (**ō**) _____ coming from the toaster while

making (**ō**) _____.

Do (**ō**) _____ live in the water like frogs?

We need to (**ī**) _____ up the nuts before we put them in the cookie dough.

Name: _____

Spelling: Long i and o

Directions: Read the words. After each word, write the correct vowel sound. Underline the letter or letters that spell the sound. The first one has been done for you.

Word	Vowel		Word	Vowel
1. br<u>i</u>ght	i		9. white	_____
2. globe	_____		10. roast	_____
3. plywood	_____		11. light	_____
4. mankind	_____		12. shallow	_____
5. coaching	_____		13. myself	_____
6. prize	_____		14. throne	_____
7. grind	_____		15. cold	_____
8. withhold	_____		16. snow	_____

Directions: Below are words written as they are pronounced. Write the words that sound like:

1. thrōn _____   5. brīt _____

2. skōld _____   6. grīnd _____

3. prīz _____   7. plīwood _____

4. rōst _____   8. mīself _____

Name:_____

Writing: Putting Ideas Together

Directions: Make each pair of sentences into one sentence. (You may have to change the verbs for some sentences—from **is** to **are**, for example.)

Example: Our house was flooded. Our car was flooded.

Our house and car were flooded.

1. Kenny sees a glow.   Carrie sees a glow.

   _____

2. Our new stove came today.   Our new refrigerator came today.

   _____

3. The pond is full of toads.   The field is full of toads.

   _____

4. Stripes are on the flag.   Stars are on the flag.

   _____

5. The ducks took flight.   The geese took flight.

   _____

6. Joe reads stories.   Dana reads stories.

   _____

7. French fries will make you fat.   Milkshakes will make you fat.

   _____

8. Justine heard someone groan.   Kevin heard someone groan.

   _____

Spelling: Plurals

Nouns come in two forms: singular and plural. When a noun is **singular**, it means there is only one person, place or thing.

Examples: car, swing, box, truck, slide, bus

When a noun is **plural**, it means there is more than one person, place or thing.

Examples: two cars, four trucks, three swings, five slides, six boxes, three buses

Usually an **s** is added to most nouns to make them plural. However, if the noun ends in **s**, **x**, **ch** or **sh**, then **es** is added to make it plural.

Directions: Write the singular or plural form of each word.

Singular	Plural		Singular	Plural
1. car	_____	9. _____		tricks
2. bush	_____	10. mess		_____
3. wish	_____	11. box		_____
4. _____	foxes	12. dish		_____
5. _____	rules	13. _____		boats
6. stitch	_____	14. path		_____
7. _____	switches	15. _____		arms
8. barn	_____	16. _____		sticks

Directions: Rewrite the following sentences and change the bold nouns from singular to plural or from plural to singular. The first one has been done for you.

1. She took a **book** to school.
   She took books to school.

2. Tommy made **wishes** at his birthday party.

   _____

3. The **fox** ran away from the hunters.

   _____

4. The **houses** were painted white.

   _____

Spelling: Plurals

When a word ends with a consonant before **y**, to make it plural, drop the **y** and add **ies**.

Examples: party   parties
                  cherry   cherries
                  daisy   daisies

However, if the word ends with a vowel before **y**, just add **s**.

Examples: boy   boys
                  toy   toys
                  monkey   monkeys

Directions: Write the singular or plural form of each word.

Singular	Plural	Singular	Plural
1. fly	_____	7. _____	decoys
2. _____	boys	8. candy	_____
3. _____	joys	9. toy	_____
4. spy	_____	10. _____	cries
5. _____	keys	11. monkey	_____
6. _____	dries	12. daisy	_____

Directions: Write six sentences of your own using any of the plurals above.

_____

_____

_____

_____

_____

_____

Name: _____

Spelling: Plurals

Some words in the English language do not follow any of the plural rules discussed earlier. These words may not change at all from singular to plural, or they may completely change spellings.

No Change	Examples:		Complete Change	Examples:	
Singular	**Plural**		**Singular**	**Plural**	
deer	deer		goose	geese	
pants	pants		ox	oxen	
scissors	scissors		man	men	
moose	moose		child	children	
sheep	sheep		leaf	leaves	

Directions: Write the singular or plural form of each word. Use a dictionary to help if necessary.

	Singular	Plural		Singular	Plural
1.	moose	_____	6.	leaf	_____
2.	woman	_____	7.	_____	sheep
3.	_____	deer	8.	scissors	_____
4.	_____	children	9.	tooth	_____
5.	_____	hooves	10.	wharf	_____

Directions: Write four sentences of your own using two singular and two plural words from above.

_____

_____

_____

_____

Review

Review these rules for making singular words plural.

For most words, simply add **s**.

Examples: one book — two books   one house — four houses

For words ending with **s**, **ss**, **sh**, **ch** and **x**, add **es**.

Examples: one class — two classes   one church — three churches
one box — four boxes   one crash — five crashes

For words ending with a consonant before **y**, drop the **y** and add **ies**.

Examples: one daisy — three daisies   one cherry — two cherries

For words ending with a vowel before **y**, just add **s**.

Examples: one key — eight keys   one monkey — four monkeys

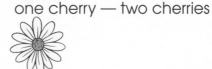

Directions: Write the singular or plural form of each word.

Singular	Plural	Singular	Plural
1. mattress	_____	10. _____	candies
2. _____	bushes	11. try	_____
3. sandwich	_____	12. _____	turkeys
4. fry	_____	13. copy	_____
5. _____	crosses	14. _____	factories
6. marsh	_____	15. _____	foxes
7. _____	supplies	16. ax	_____
8. donkey	_____	17. berry	_____
9. _____	stoves	18. day	_____

39

Writing: Adjectives

Adjectives tell more about nouns. Adjectives are describing words.

Examples: scary animals   **bright** glow   **wet** frog

Directions: Add at least two adjectives to each sentence below. Use your own words or words from the box.

pale	soft	sticky	burning	furry	glistening	peaceful
faint	shivering	slippery	gleaming	gentle	foggy	tangled

Example: The stripe was blue.
The wide stripe was light blue.

1. The frog had eyes.

   _____

2. The house was a sight.

   _____

3. A boy heard a noise.

   _____

4. The girl tripped over a toad.

   _____

5. A tiger ran through the room.

   _____

6. They saw a glow in the window.

   _____

7. A pan was sitting on the stove.

   _____

8. The boys were eating French fries.

   _____

Name: _____

Writing: Adjectives

Adjectives tell a noun's size, color, shape, texture, brightness, darkness, personality, sound, taste, and so on.

Examples: color — red, yellow, green, black
size — small, large, huge, tiny
shape — round, square, rectangular, oval
texture — rough, smooth, soft, scaly
brightness — glistening, shimmering, dull, pale
personality — gentle, grumpy, happy, sad

Directions: Follow the instructions below.

1. Get an apple, orange or other piece of fruit. Look at it very carefully and write adjectives that describe its size, color, shape and texture.

    _____

    _____

2. Take a bite of your fruit. Write adjectives that describe its taste, texture, smell, and so on.

    _____

    _____

3. Using all the adjectives from above, write a cinquain about your fruit. A **cinquain** is a five-line poem. See the form and sample poem below.

    Form: Line 1 — noun
    Line 2 — two adjectives
    Line 3 — three sounds
    Line 4 — four-word phrase
    Line 5 — noun

    Example: Apple

    red, smooth

    cracking, smacking, slurping

    drippy, sticky, sour juice

    Apple

    _____

    _____ , _____

    _____ , _____ , _____

    _____

    _____

Spelling: Long u

Long **ū** can be spelled, **u-e** as in **cube** or **ew** as in **few**. Some sounds are similar in sound to **u** but are not true **u** sounds, such as the **oo** in **tooth**, the **o-e** in **move** and the **ue** in **blue**.

Directions: Complete each sentence using a word from the box. Do not use the same word more than once.

blew

tune

flute

cute

stew

June

glue

1. Yesterday, the wind _____ so hard it knocked down a tree on our street.

2. My favorite instrument is the _____.

3. The little puppy in the window is so _____.

4. I love _____ because it's so warm, and we get out of school.

5. For that project, you will need scissors, construction paper and _____.

6. I recognize that song because it has a familiar _____.

7. My grandmother's beef _____ is the best I've ever tasted.

Writing: Adverbs

Like adjectives, **adverbs** are describing words. They describe verbs. Adverbs tell how, when or where action takes place.

Examples: How	When	Where
slowly	yesterday	here
gracefully	today	there
swiftly	tomorrow	everywhere
quickly	soon	

Hint: To identify an adverb, locate the verb, then ask yourself if there are any words that tell how, when or where action takes place.

Directions: Read the following sentences. Underline the adverbs, then write whether they tell how, when or where. The first one has been done for you.

1. At the end of the day, the children ran quickly home from school.   _____how_____

2. They will have a spelling test tomorrow.   _____

3. Slowly, the children filed to their seats.   _____

4. The teacher sat here at her desk.   _____

5. She will pass the tests back later.   _____

6. The students received their grades happily.   _____

Directions: Write four sentences of your own using any of the adverbs above.

_____

_____

_____

_____

Name:_____

Writing: Using Adjectives and Adverbs

Directions: Complete these sentences by adding words that tell who, what, where or when.

Who or What		Where	When
tiger	stripe	out of sight	early in the morning
someone	groan	behind the door	when I wasn't looking
friend	glow	far away	late at night
sister	toad	very close	before I got there
brother	stove	up the stairs	when the moon was full

Example: They noticed a green glow behind the pine trees.
                    (what)   (where)

1. _____ shifted across the room _____.
      (who or what)   (when)

2. The shadow covered _____.
                         (what)   (where)

3. The door _____ opened _____.
                (where)   (when)

4. _____ hurried _____.
   (who or what)   (where)   (when)

5. _____ stopped the _____.
   (who or what)   (what)   (when)

Name: _____

Spelling: Vowel Sound Puzzle

Directions: Write the word from the box that answers each question.

| stripe | groan | toast | grind | fly | sight | stove | tune | flight |

Across:

Which word . . .
2. Begins like **toe** and rhymes with **most**?
4. Sounds the same as **grown**?
5. Begins like **stop** and rhymes with **cove**?
6. Begins like **flip** and rhymes with **kite**?

Down:

Which word . . .
1. Begins like **green** and rhymes with **find**?
2. Begins like **to** and rhymes with **moon**?
3. Begins like **stop** and rhymes with **type**?
5. Begins like **season** and rhymes with **bite**?
6. Begins like **feather** and rhymes with **pie**?

Name: _____

Review

Directions: Circle the letters that spell three ō vowels, three ī vowels and one ū vowel in the sentence below.

Mike hopes his cute toad will be home by tonight.

Directions: Pretend something scary happened and you are asked to write about it for your school newspaper.

Follow these steps:

1. Write all your ideas in any order on another sheet of paper. What could have happened? Where? Why was it scary? Who was there? What did he or she do?

2. Choose the ideas you want to use and put them in order.

3. Now, write what happened in sentences, using as many adjectives and plurals as you can. Combine some of the sentences.

4. Read your sentences aloud. Will your readers understand what happened? Do you need to make any changes?

5. After you make any necessary changes, write your article below.

6. Draw a picture to help you show what happened.

7. Show someone your article and picture.

Title of Article: _____

_____

_____

_____

_____

_____

_____

_____

Spelling: The k Sound

The **k** sound can be spelled with **k** as in **peek**, **c** as in **cousin**, **ck** as in **sick**, **ch** as in **Chris** and **cc** as in **accuse**. In some words, however, one **c** may be pronounced **k** and the other **s** as in **accident**.

Directions: Answer the questions with words from the box.

Christmas	freckles	command	cork	jacket
accused	castle	stomach	rake	accident

1. Which two words spell **k** with just a **k**?

   _____   _____

2. Which two words spell **k** with **ck**?

   _____   _____

3. Which two words spell **k** with **ch**?

   _____   _____

4. Which four words spell **k** with **c** or **cc**?

   _____   _____

   _____   _____

5. Complete these sentences, using a word with **k** spelled as shown. Use each word from the box only once.

   Dad gave Mom a garden (**k**) _____ for (**ch**) _____.

   There are (**ck**) _____ on my face and (**ch**) _____.

   The people (**cc**) _____ her of taking a (**ck**) _____.

   The police took (**c**) _____ after the (**cc**) _____.

   The model of the (**c**) _____ was made out of

   (**c and k**) _____.

Name: _____

Spelling: The k Sound

Directions: Underline the letters that spell **k** in each word. The first one has been done for you.

1. toothpi**ck**

2. arc

3. kitchen

4. acclaim

5. account

6. Christmas

7. make

8. confirm

9. brick

10. stomach

toothpick
c – k

Directions: Under each spelling for **k**, write five words that have the same **k** spellings.

k	ck	c	ch	cc
	sickness			
			chemical	
		candy		
				accumulate
kite				

Directions: See how many words you can write that have the **cc** spelling, with one **c** pronounced **k** and the other pronounced **s**.

_____

_____

_____

Name:_____

Writing: Using Conjunctions

Conjunctions are joining words that can be used to combine sentences. Words such as **and**, **but**, **or**, **when** and **after** are conjunctions.

Examples:
Sally went to the mall. She went to the movies.
Sally went to the mall, and she went to the movies.

We can have our vacation at home. We can vacation at the beach.
We can have our vacation at home, or we can vacation at the beach.

Mary fell on the playground. She did not hurt herself.
Mary fell on the playground, but she did not hurt herself.

Note: The conjunctions **after** or **when** are usually placed at the beginning of the sentence.

Example: Marge went to the store. She went to the gas station.
   After Marge went to the store, she went to the gas station.

Directions: Combine the following sentences using a conjunction.

1. Peter fell down the steps. He broke his foot. (and)

_____

2. I visited New York. I would like to see Chicago. (but)

_____

3. Amy can edit books. She can write stories. (or)

_____

4. He played in the barn. John started to sneeze. (when)

_____

5. The team won the playoffs. They went to the championships. (after)

_____

Directions: Write three sentences of your own using the conjunctions **and**, **but**, **or**, **when** or **after**.

_____

_____

_____

_____

Name:_____

Writing: Using Conjunctions

Directions: Combine each pair of sentences using the conjunctions **or**, **and**, **but**, **after** or **when**. You may need to change the word order in the sentences.

Examples:

My stomach hurts.   I still want to go to the movies.

My stomach hurts, but I still want to go to the movies.

1. He accused me of peeking.   I felt very angry.

    _____

2. The accident was over.   I started shaking.

    _____

3. Is that a freckle?   Is that dirt?

    _____

4. I forgot my jacket.   I had to go back and get it.

    _____

5. I like Christmas.   I don't like waiting for it.

    _____

6. Would you like to live in a castle?   Would you like to live on a houseboat?

    _____

7. The general gave the command.   The army marched.

    _____

8. The trees dropped all their leaves.   We raked them up.

    _____

Name: _____

Writing: Using ing Verbs

Remember, use **is** and **are** when describing something happening right now. Use **was** and **were** when describing something that already happened.

Directions: Use the verb on the left to complete each sentence. Add **ing** to the verb and use **is**, **are**, **was** or **were**.

Examples:
When it started to rain, we <u>were raking</u>
the leaves.   **rake**

When the soldiers marched up that hill,

Captain Stevens <u>was commanding</u> them.
            command

1. Now, the police _____ them of stealing the money.
            accuse

2. Look! The eggs _____.
            hatch

3. A minute ago, the sky _____.
            glow

4. My dad says he _____ us to ice cream!
            treat

5. She _____ the whole time we were at the mall.
            sneeze

6. While we were playing outside at recess, he _____
   our tests.   **grade**

7. I hear something. Who _____?
            groan

8. As I watched, the workers _____ the wood into
   little chips.   **grind**

Name: _____

Writing: Using ing Verbs

Using **ing** verbs can make your writing more interesting to read. Compare these lists of verbs:

List A
went
look
find
sleep
run
drop
go

List B
skipping
discovering
digging
snoring
slithering
sailing
soaring

Now, compare these sentences. Notice that the second sentence is much more descriptive.

The children went home from school.
The children were flying out the school doors.

Directions: Change each bold verb to a more descriptive **ing** verb. Don't forget to add a helping verb (**am**, **is**, **are**, **was**, **were**).

1. The snake **went** among the rocks.

   _____

2. Water **fell** over the cliff.

   _____

3. The leaves **drop** to the ground.

   _____

4. Snowflakes **fall** from the sky.

   _____

5. At the library, she **looked** for a book.

   _____

6. Her horse got loose and **ran** across the meadow.

   _____

7. Min **laughed** at the clown's tricks.

   _____

Name: _____

Writing: Using ing Verbs

Directions: Using descriptive **ing** verbs, write five sentences about activities you do every day.

Example: Peter ate his breakfast.
Peter is scarfing down his breakfast so he won't miss the bus.

_____

_____

_____

_____

_____

Directions: Use **ing** verbs to write a cinquain. Then draw a picture to go with it.

Form

noun
two adjectives
three **ing** verbs
four-word phrase
noun

Example:

Snowflake
feathery, soft
twirling, swirling, floating
no two are alike
Crystal

_____

_____ , _____

_____ , _____ , _____

_____

_____

Name:_____

Writing: Using Conjunctions

Directions: Combine each pair of sentences, choosing the best joining words. Here are some choices: **and**, **but**, **or**, **when** and **after**. You may need to change the sentence order.

1. I would like to live in a castle.   There aren't any in our neighborhood.

_____

2. I sit in the sun.   I get more freckles.

_____

3. The teacher gives a command.   Everyone changes places.

_____

4. Does cork come from trees?   Is it man-made?

_____

5. I tried on my old jacket.   It still fits.

_____

6. Christmas was over.   We took down our tree.

_____

7. I took my medicine.   My stomach felt much better.

_____

8. I'd like to rake the leaves.   It's raining now.

_____

Name: _____

Spelling: Finding Mistakes

Directions: Circle the spelling mistakes. Then write the words correctly.

1. What did you get for Cristmas this year? _____

2. My aunt gave me boots and a new jaket. _____

3. I need to get some food in my stomack. _____

4. Does anyone know why korks float? _____

5. I dropped my glass by acident. _____

6. A comand is a sentence that tells someone to do something. _____

7. We visited a casel on our trip to Ireland. _____

8. My big brother is always acusing me of using his stuff. _____

9. I lost the rak under all the leaves. _____

10. I wish I had as many frekles as you. _____

Make up five sentences using a **k** word in each. Spell the **k** word incorrectly and see if someone else can find the mistake.

_____

_____

_____

_____

_____

Name: _____

Writing: Punctuation

Directions: In the paragraphs below, use periods, question marks or exclamation marks to show where one sentence ends and the next begins. Circle the first letter of each new sentence to show the capital.

Example: (m)y sister accused me of not helping her rake the leaves. (t)hat's silly! (i) helped at least a hundred times.

1. I always tie on my fishing line when it moves up and down, I know a fish is there after waiting a minute or two, I pull up the fish it's fun

2. I tried putting lemon juice on my freckles to make them go away did you ever do that it didn't work my skin just got sticky now, I'm slowly getting used to my freckles

3. once, I had an accident on my bike I was on my way home from school what do you think happened my wheel slipped in the loose dirt at the side of the road my bike slid into the road

4. one night, I dreamed I lived in a castle in my dream, I was the king or maybe the queen everyone listened to my commands then Mom woke me up for school I tried commanding her to let me sleep it didn't work

5. what's your favorite holiday Christmas is mine for months before Christmas, I save my money, so I can give a present to everyone in my family last year, I gave my big sister earrings they cost me five dollars

6. my dad does exercises every night to make his stomach flat he says he doesn't want to grow old I think it's too late don't tell him I said that

Writing: Punctuation

Directions: In the paragraphs below, use periods, question marks and exclamation marks to show where one sentence ends and the next begins. Circle the first letter of each new sentence to show the capital.

1. It was Christmas Eve Santa and the elves were loading the toys onto his sleigh the deer keepers were harnessing the reindeer and walking them toward the sleigh

2. the reindeer were prancing with anxious anticipation of their midnight flight soon, the sleigh was overflowing with its load, and Santa was ready to travel crack went his whip the reindeer pulled and tugged against their harnesses the sleigh inched forward, slowly at first, then swiftly it climbed into the holiday night sky

3. everything was going smoothly Santa and the reindeer made excellent time traveling from house to house and city to city at each home, of course, the children had left Santa snacks of cookies and milk

4. around 2 o'clock in the morning, Santa felt his red suit begin to get tight around his middle "hmm," he said to himself "I have been eating too many snacks" he decided that after the next house he would have to cut back on his cookie calories

5. the reindeer team guided Santa to his next stop he hopped out of his sleigh, grabbed his bundle of toys and jogged to the chimney he climbed up to the chimney's opening and started down to the fireplace oops something awful happened Santa got stuck oh, no what do we do now wondered the reindeer

Directions: Complete the story about Santa. Use your knowledge of adjectives, adverbs and descriptive verbs to make your story more interesting and fun to read.

Spelling: Figuring Out the Code

Remember that the vowels are **a, e, i, o, u** and sometimes **y**. All the other letters are consonants.

Directions: Each picture below stands for a consonant. Write the consonant it stands for on the line. Then add vowels to spell words from the box.

= c   = h   = r   = d   = m

= s   = k   = n   = t

| ~~cork~~ | ~~accuse~~ | stomach | ~~rake~~ | ~~command~~ |

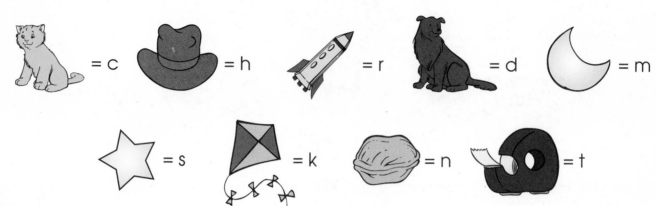

Example:

r   k   rake

1. C _____ K _____   cork

2. _____   accuse

3. _____   command

4. _____   stomach

Name:_____

Writing: Story Map

A **story map** helps to organize your thoughts in a logical sequence before you begin to write a story or report.

Directions: Use the following story map to arrange your thoughts for the police report on page 60.

Characters:

Setting: (time, place)

Problem: (what needs to be fixed or solved)

Goal: (what characters want to accomplish)

Action: (events, reasons)

Outcome: (results of action)

Name: _____

Review

Directions: Write a police report about an event in which someone your age was a hero or heroine. Follow these steps:

1. Write all your ideas in any order on another sheet of paper. What happened? Who saw it? Who or what do you think caused it? Why were the police called?

2. Choose the ideas you want to use and organize them with the story map on page 59.

3. Now, write in complete sentences to tell what happened. Combine some short sentences using **and**, **but**, **or**, **after** or **when**. Make sure all your sentences end with a period or question mark.

4. Read your sentences aloud. Did you leave out any important facts? Will your "commanding officer" know what happened?

5. Make any necessary changes and write your report below.

6. Read your report to someone.

OFFICIAL POLICE REPORT

Reporting officer: _____

Date of accident: _____ Time of accident: _____

_____

_____

_____

_____

_____

_____

_____

_____

Name: _____

Spelling: The f Sound

The **f** sound can be spelled with **f** as in **fun**, **gh** as in **laugh** or **ph** as in **phone**.

Directions: Answer the questions with words from the box.

fuss	paragraph	phone	friendship	freedom
defend	flood	alphabet	rough	laughter

1. Which three words spell **f** with **ph**?

   _____   _____   _____

2. Which two words spell **f** with **gh**?

   _____   _____

3. Which five words spell **f** with an **f**?

   _____   _____   _____

   _____   _____

4. Complete these sentences, using a word with **f** spelled as shown. Use each word from the box only once.

   I don't know why my teacher makes so much (**f**) _____ over writing

   a (**ph**) _____.

   A (**f**) _____ can help you through (**gh**) _____ times.

   The soldiers will (**f**) _____ our (**f**) _____.

   Can you say the (**ph**) _____ backwards?

   When I answered the (**ph**) _____, all I could

   hear was (**gh**) _____.

   If it keeps raining, we'll have a (**f**) _____.

Name: _____

Spelling: The f Sound

Directions: Read the following words. Underline the letters that spell **f** in each word.

1. laughter
2. football
3. cough
4. paragraph
5. enough

6. phantom
7. roof
8. performance
9. toughest
10. telephone

11. before
12. roughness
13. alphabet
14. grief
15. graph

Directions: Under each spelling for the **f** sound, write five words with the same **f** letter or letters. Use words other than those above.

f	gh	ph
_____	_____	_____
_____	_____	_____
_____	_____	_____
_____	_____	_____
_____	_____	_____

Name: _____

Writing: Topic Sentences

A **paragraph** is a group of sentences that tells about one main idea. A **topic sentence** tells the main idea of a paragraph.

Many topic sentences come first in the paragraph. The topic sentence in the paragraph below is underlined. Do you see how it tells the reader what the whole paragraph is about?

Friendships can make you happy or make you sad. You feel happy to do things and go places with your friends. You get to know each other so well that you can almost read each others' minds. But friendships can be sad when your friend moves away—or decides to be best friends with someone else.

Directions: Underline the topic sentence in the paragraph below.

We have two rules about using the phone at our house. Our whole family agreed on them. The first rule is not to talk longer than 10 minutes. The second rule is to take good messages if you answer the phone for someone else.

Directions: After you read the paragraph below, write a topic sentence for it.

_____

_____

_____

_____

For one thing, you could ask your neighbors if they need any help. They might be willing to pay you for walking their dog or mowing their grass or weeding their garden. Maybe your older brothers or sisters would pay you to do some of their chores. You also could ask your parents if there's an extra job you could do around the house to make money.

Directions: Write a topic sentence for a paragraph on each of these subjects.

Homework: _____

_____

Television: _____

_____

Name: _____

Writing: Supporting Sentences

Supporting sentences provide details about the topic sentence of a paragraph.

Directions: In the paragraph below, underline the topic sentence. Then cross out the supporting sentence that does not belong in the paragraph.

One spring it started to rain and didn't stop for 2 weeks. All the rivers flooded. Some people living near the rivers had to leave their homes. Farmers couldn't plant their crops because the fields were so wet. Plants need water to grow. The sky was dark and gloomy all the time.

Directions: Write three supporting sentences to go with each topic sentence below. Make sure each supporting sentence stays on the same subject as the topic sentence.

Not everyone should have a pet.

_____

_____

_____

I like to go on field trips with my class.

_____

_____

_____

I've been thinking about what I want to be when I get older.

_____

_____

_____

Name: _____

Writing:
Topic Sentences and Supporting Details

Directions: For each topic below, write a topic sentence and four supporting details.

Example:

Playing with friends: (topic sentence) <u>Playing with my friends can be lots of fun.</u>

(details)

1. We like to ride our bikes together.

2. We play fun games like "dress up" and "animal hospital."

3. Sometimes, we swing on the swings or slide down the slides on our swingsets.

4. We like to pretend we are having tea with our stuffed animals.

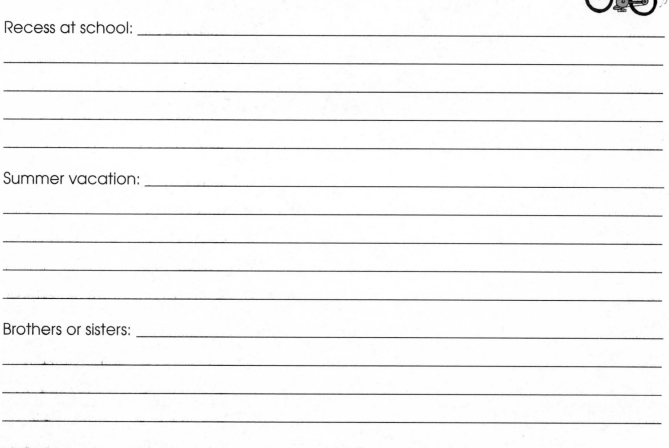

Recess at school: _____

_____

_____

_____

_____

Summer vacation: _____

_____

_____

_____

_____

Brothers or sisters: _____

_____

_____

_____

_____

Name: _____

Writing:
Topic Sentences and Supporting Details

Directions: Select a topic from page 65. Arrange the topic sentence and detail sentences in paragraph form.

Example: Playing With Friends

    Playing with my friends can be lots of fun. We play fun games like animal hospital and "dress up." We like to pretend we are having tea with our stuffed animals. Sometimes, we swing on the swings or slide down the slides on our swingsets. We also like to ride our bikes together.

Note: Notice how the first line of the paragraph is indented. Also note how the order of the sentences changed to make the paragraph easier to read.

Directions: Choose a topic. Write a five-sentence paragraph about it. Don't forget the topic sentence, supporting details and to indent your paragraph. Make sure the detail sentences stick to the topic.

_____

_____

_____

_____

_____

_____

Name:_____

Spelling: Syllables

A **syllable** is a word—or part of a word—with only one vowel sound. Some words have just one syllable, such as **cat**, **dog** and **house**. Some words have two syllables, such as **in-sist** and **be-fore**. Some words have three syllables, such as **re-mem-ber**; four syllables, such as **un-der-stand-ing**; or more. Often words are easier to spell if you know how many syllables they have.

Syl-la-bles

Directions: Write the number of syllables in each word below.

Word	Syllables		Word	Syllables
1. amphibian	_____		11. want	_____
2. liter	_____		12. communication	_____
3. guild	_____		13. pedestrian	_____
4. chili	_____		14. kilo	_____
5. vegetarian	_____		15. autumn	_____
6. comedian	_____		16. dinosaur	_____
7. warm	_____		17. grammar	_____
8. piano	_____		18. dry	_____
9. barbarian	_____		19. solar	_____
10. chef	_____		20. wild	_____

Directions: Next to each number, write words with the same number of syllables.

1 _____ _____ _____ _____

2 _____ _____ _____

3 _____ _____ _____

4 _____ _____ _____

5 _____ _____

Name: _____

Spelling: Syllables

Directions: Write each word from the box next to the number that shows how many syllables it has.

fuss	paragraph	phone	friendship	freedom
defend	flood	alphabet	rough	laughter

One: _____ _____ _____ _____

Two: _____ _____ _____ _____

Three: _____ _____

How many syllables are there in the word **friendship**?

Directions: Circle the two words in each row that have the same number of syllables as the first word.

Example: fact	clay	happy	phone	command
rough	freckle	pump	accuse	ghost
jacket	flood	laughter	defend	paragraph
accident	paragraph	carpenter	stomach	castle
comfort	agree	friend	friendship	health
fuss	collect	blend	freedom	hatch
alphabet	thankful	Christmas	enemy	unhappy
glowing	midnight	defending	grading	telephone

Spelling: Searching for Words

Directions: Make a word search using words from the box. First, print the words in the spaces below, making some of them cross each other. Then fill the extra spaces with other letters.

Example:

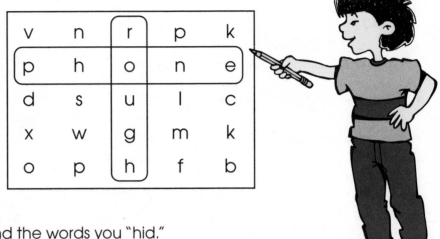

v	n	r	p	k
p	h	o	n	e
d	s	u	l	c
x	w	g	m	k
o	p	h	f	b

See if someone else can find the words you "hid."

fuss	paragraph	phone	friendship	freedom
defend	flood	alphabet	rough	laughter

Name: _____

Writing: Paragraphs

Each paragraph should have one main idea. If you have a lot of ideas, you need to write several paragraphs.

Directions: Read the ideas below and number them:
1. If the idea tells about Jill herself.
2. If the idea tells what she did.
3. If the idea tells why she did it.

_____ found a bird caught in a kite string

_____ plays outside a lot

_____ in grade four at Center School

_____ knew the bird was wild

_____ untangled the bird

_____ likes pets

_____ wouldn't want to live in a cage

_____ gave the bird its freedom

Now, use the ideas to write three paragraphs. Use your own paper if necessary. Write paragraph 1 about Jill. Write paragraph 2 about what she did. Write paragraph 3 about why she did it.

_____

_____

_____

_____

_____

_____

_____

_____

Name: _____

Writing: Paragraphs

When you have many good ideas about a subject, you need to organize your writing into more than one paragraph. It is easy to organize your thoughts about a topic if you use a "cluster of ideas" chart.

Example:

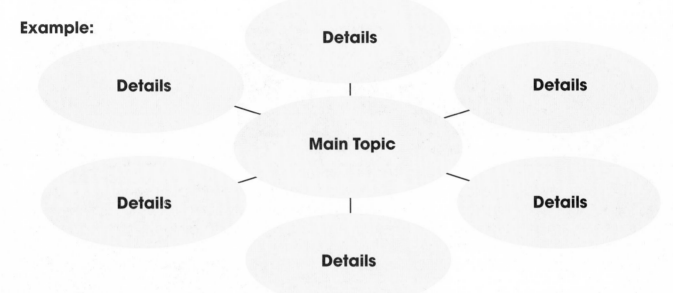

The main topic of your story is stated in the middle circle. Details about the main topic are listed in the outer circles.

Study the following "cluster of ideas" and note how the thoughts are organized in paragraph form on the following page.

1. **Introduction:** working in yard, autumn—cool weather

2. **Pants:** blue jeans, old, cotton, good for yard work, comfortable

3. **Shirt:** yellow, short-sleeved, matches slacks and sweater, not too hot

Clothes for Saturday

4. **Sweater:** red with yellow and blue designs, white buttons, warmth for cold day, cotton, long sleeves

5. **Shoes:** white sneakers, comfortable, good for walking and standing

6. **Closing:** busy, but ready

Name: _____

Writing: Paragraphs

Once your ideas are "clustered," go back and decide which ideas should be the first, second, third, and so on. These numbers will be the order of the paragraph in the finished story.

Directions: Read the story paragraphs below.

Clothes for Saturday

This Saturday, my family and I will be working in the yard. We will be mowing grass, raking leaves and pulling weeds. When I get up that day, I know I will need to wear clothes that will keep me warm in the autumn air. My clothes will also need to be ones that will not be ruined if they get muddy or dirty.

The best choice of pants for our busy day will be my jeans. They are nicely faded and well worn, which means they are quite comfortable. They will be good for yard work since mud and grass stains wash out of them easily.

My shirt will be my yellow golf shirt. It will match the blue of my jeans. Also, its short sleeves will be fine if the weather is warm.

For warmth on Saturday, if the day is cool, will be my yellow and red sweater. It is made from cotton and has long sleeves and high buttons to keep out frosty air.

Yard work means lots of walking, so I will need comfortable shoes. The best choice will be my white sneakers. They aren't too tight or too loose and keep my feet strong.

Saturday will be a busy day, but I'll be ready!

When "Clothes for Saturday" was written, the author added both an introductory and concluding paragraph. This helps the reader with the flow of the story.

Directions: Now, it's your turn. Select a topic from the list below or choose one of your own. Complete the "cluster of ideas" chart on page 73 and write a brief story. (You may or may not use all the clusters.)

Topics:

chores	holidays	all about me	sports
homework	family	pets	vacation

Name: _____

Writing: Cluster of Ideas

Details

Details

Details

Main Topic

Details

Details

Details

_____

_____

_____

_____

_____

_____

_____

_____

_____

_____

_____

_____

Name: _____

Spelling: Unscrambling Letters

Directions: Put the letters in order to spell the **f** words. If you need help with spelling, look on page 61.

feeddn   _____   odolf   _____

nopeh   _____   dspiienfhr   _____

gletharu   _____   gruho   _____

ssfu   _____   taalbehp   _____

droefem   _____   ghaaprpar   _____

RT UAHP GBLRT

Directions: Use the correctly spelled word to answer the questions.

1. Which two words each have one syllable and spell **f** with an **f**?

_____

2. Which word has two syllables and spells **f** with **gh**? _____

3. Which word has one syllable and spells **f** with **ph**? _____

4. Which three words each have two syllables and spell **f** with an **f**?

_____

5. Which two words each have three syllables and spell **f** with a **ph**?

_____

6. Which word has one syllable and spells **f** with **gh**? _____

Name: _____

Review

Directions: On another sheet of paper, write three paragraphs that tell a story about the picture below. Tell who lives in the house, what happened and why it happened. Begin each paragraph with a topic sentence that tells the main idea. Try to include some words with the **f** sound in them. Read your paragraphs aloud, make any necessary changes and copy them below.

Who lives there:

_____

_____

_____

What happened:

_____

_____

_____

Why it happened:

_____

_____

_____

Name: _____

Spelling: The s Sound

The **s** sound can be spelled with **s** as in **super** or **ss** as in **assign**, **c** as in **city**, **ce** as in **fence** or **sc** as in **scene**. In some words, though, **sc** is pronounced **sk**, as in **scare**.

Directions: Answer the questions using words from the box.

exciting	medicine	lettuce	peace	scissors
slice	scientist	sauce	bracelet	distance

1. Which five words spell **s** with just an **s** or **ss**?

   _____   _____

   _____   _____

2. Which two words spell **s** with just a **c**?

   _____   _____

3. Which six words spell **s** with a **ce**?

   _____   _____

   _____   _____

4. Which two words spell **s** with **sc**?

   _____   _____

5. Complete these sentences, using a word with **s** spelled as shown. Use each word from the box only once.

   My (**ce**) _____ fell off my wrist into the tomato

   _____ (**s and ce**).

   My salad was just a (**s and ce**) _____ of (**ce**) _____.

   It was (**c**) _____ to see the lions, even though they were a long

   (**s and ce**) _____ away.

   The (**sc and s**) _____ invented a new (**c**) _____.

   If I lend you my (**sc and ss**) _____, will you leave me in

   (**ce**) _____?

Name: _____

Spelling: The s Sound

Directions: Read the following words. Underline the letters that spell **s** in each word. In some words, more than one letter will be underlined.

1. impassive
2. placement
3. question
4. conscious
5. excellence
6. assertive
7. scepter
8. scoundrel

9. assortment
10. ignorance
11. precious
12. judicious
13. difference
14. lifeless
15. solvent
16. scope

17. castle
18. scamper
19. sociable
20. amusement
21. scissors
22. insurance
23. scamp
24. science

Ssss. . . .Ssss. . . .Ssss. . . .Ssss!

Directions: Under each spelling for **s**, write five words with the same **s** letters. Use words other than those above.

s or ss	c	ce	sc

Name: _____

Writing: Cause and Effect

Sometimes one sentence names an **effect** (something that happens) and another sentence tells what caused it. The **cause** is the reason something happens. Use the word **because** to combine them.

Example:
He was crying. (effect)
He fell off his bike. (cause)
He was crying because he fell off his bike.

Directions: Draw a line from each effect on the left to its cause on the right.

1. I didn't finish my project   because I like to experiment.

2. I have to take medicine   because today is her birthday.

3. I want to be a scientist   because I can't find scissors.

4. I gave my sister a bracelet   because my throat hurts.

The cause can also be written and combined with the word **so**.

Example:
Today is my sister's birthday, so I gave her a bracelet.
   (cause)   (effect)

Directions: Write the other three sentences from above with the cause first.

1. _____

   _____

2. _____

   _____

3. _____

   _____

Name: _____

Spelling: Listening for Sounds and Syllables

Directions: Answer the questions using words from the box.

| exciting | medicine | lettuce | peace | scissors |
| slice | scientist | sauce | bracelet | distance |

1. Which three words have only one syllable?

   _____ _____ _____

2. Which four words have two syllables?

   _____ _____

   _____ _____

3. Which three words have three syllables?

   _____ _____ _____

4. Which three words start with the same sound as **center** and end with the same sound as **dance**?

   _____ _____ _____

5. Which word begins with the same sound as
   dance and ends with the same sound as **pass**? _____

6. Which word begins with the same sound as **pass**
   and ends with the same sound as **surface**? _____

7. Which word begins with the same sound as
   surface and ends with the same sound as **late**? _____

8. Which word begins with the same sound as **late**
   and ends with the same sound as **bus**? _____

9. Which word begins with the same sound as **bus**
   and ends with the same sound as **late**? _____

Name:_____

Writing: Writing Sentences Two Ways

Directions: Combine each pair of sentences in two ways. Write the cause first, then the effect first.

Example: Please buy more lettuce. Aunt Ethel likes salad.

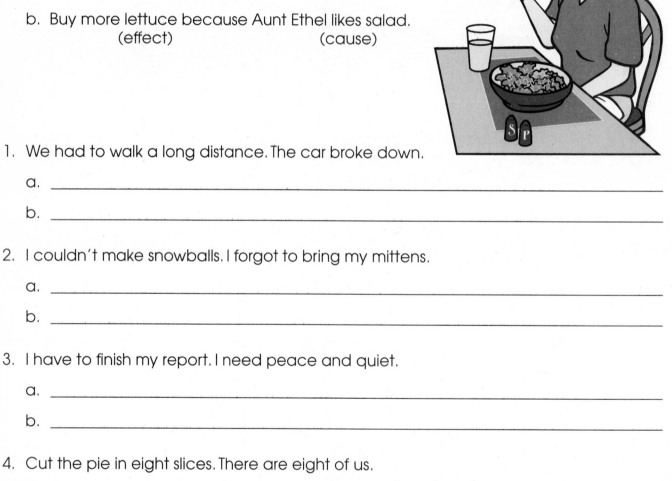

   a. Aunt Ethel likes salad, so buy more lettuce.
       (cause)   (effect)

   b. Buy more lettuce because Aunt Ethel likes salad.
       (effect)   (cause)

1. We had to walk a long distance. The car broke down.

   a. _____

   b. _____

2. I couldn't make snowballs. I forgot to bring my mittens.

   a. _____

   b. _____

3. I have to finish my report. I need peace and quiet.

   a. _____

   b. _____

4. Cut the pie in eight slices. There are eight of us.

   a. _____

   b. _____

5. We are out of cheese sauce. I will make some more.

   a. _____

   b. _____

Writing: Cause and Effect

Directions: Add a cause to each sentence.

Example: The nations were at peace **because the war was finally over**.

1. Mike's story was exciting _____
   _____.

2. Anna couldn't cut her cake in slices _____
   _____.

3. I asked Mom for some medicine _____
   _____.

4. I don't like lettuce _____
   _____.

Directions: Add an effect to each sentence.

Example: The scientist was distracted, **so he made a mistake**.

1. I had run for a long distance _____
   _____.

2. The sauce cooked too long _____
   _____.

3. Ryan's scissors were dull _____
   _____.

4. The bracelet was expensive _____
   _____.

Name:_____

Spelling: Possessives

A **possessive noun** shows that something belongs to the noun. To show possession with singular nouns, an **apostrophe** and **s** are usually added.

Examples: Doug**'s** coat   dog**'s** leg

To show possession with a plural noun that ends with **s**, place an apostrophe after the **s**.

Examples: girl**s'** papers   bird**s'** food

To show possession with a plural noun that doesn't end with **s**, add an apostrophe and **s**.

Examples: men**'s** shirts   mice**'s** hole

Directions: Write the form of the word that is missing.

Singular	Singular Possessive	Plural	Plural Possessive
_____	horse's	_____	horses'
girl	_____	girls	_____
mouse	_____	_____	mice's
fish	_____	_____	fish's
_____	baby's	babies	_____
_____	child's	_____	children's
man	_____	men	_____

Directions: Complete the sentences with the correct form of the given word.

1. (Julie)   What happened to _____ slice of cake?

2. (mother)   Did you taste my _____ sauce?

3. (child)   The library has many exciting _____ books.

Name: _____

Spelling: Telling Plurals From Possessives

Remember: A noun is possessive when something belongs to it. A plural refers to more than one thing.

Examples: girl**s**   branch**es**   fox**es**

You also know we show possession by adding:
- an apostrophe and **s** to singular nouns: girl**'s** child**'s**
- just an apostrophe to plural nouns that end in **s**: girl**s'**
- an apostrophe and **s** to plural nouns that don't end in **s**: children**'s** women**'s**

Directions: In each pair of sentences below, the given word should be plural in one and plural possessive in the other. Decide which is which and write the correct forms.

Example: (girls)   The <u>girls</u> decided to return to camp. The <u>girls'</u> tent had blown down.

1. (boys)   Please refill the _____ glasses.

   Did the _____ say when they were coming?

2. (reporters)   _____ shouldn't misspell words.

   Where are the _____ notes?

3. (teachers)   Where will the _____ eat?

   Did you misplace the _____ lunches?

4. (men)   Two _____ were unable to lift it.

   The _____ ride was late.

5. (scientists)   The _____ report was full of facts.

   The _____ had many opinions.

6. (children)   It's time to call the _____.

   Did you read the _____ stories?

Spelling: S Sound Crossword Puzzle

Directions: Complete the puzzle below with **s** words.

Across:

2. Something that cuts
6. A long way
7. Poured over spaghetti
8. Something fun and interesting
9. The opposite of **war**

Down:

1. A person who makes discoveries
3. Jewelry that fits on your wrist
4. Sometimes helps to cure illness
5. Green and leafy vegetable
7. A thin piece

Name:_____

Review

Directions: Follow these steps to complete the story:

1. Read the beginning of the story below and think about what might happen next. These ideas may help you get started:
   She decided to take a slice of . . .
   She was worried about what might happen, so . . .
   Later she found out it worked as medicine for . . .
   Her discovery was exciting because . . .
   People came great distances to . . .

2. Write ideas for your story on another sheet of paper.

3. Choose the ideas you want to use and group them into paragraphs, with one main idea in each paragraph.

4. Write the story in sentences. Remember to combine some of the sentences that explain cause and effect. Use a possessive noun at least twice.

5. Read your story aloud. Is it clear what happened? Are your ideas in order? Does your story have an ending?

6. Write your story below, using more paper if needed.

7. Let someone read your story.

   One day, by accident, a scientist named Susan dropped some lettuce from her sandwich into a special experiment. As Susan watched, . . .

_____

_____

_____

_____

_____

_____

_____

_____

_____

Name: _____

Spelling: Prefixes

A **prefix** is a syllable added to the beginning of a word that changes its meaning.
The prefix **un** means "not." **Unmade** means "not made."
The prefix **re** means "back" or "again." **Return** means "turn back."
The prefix **mis** means "wrong." **Mispronounce** means "pronounce wrong."

Directions: Add each prefix to the word to form
a new word. Then write what the new word means.

Example:	**Words**	**Meaning**
un + known =	unknown	not known
re + place =	_____	_____
mis + spell =	_____	_____
un + able =	_____	_____
re + pay =	_____	_____
mis + use =	_____	_____
un + usual =	_____	_____
re + view =	_____	_____
mis + place =	_____	_____
re + fill =	_____	_____
un + sure =	_____	_____

Directions: Add **un**, **re** or **mis** to each given word.

1. It's (usual) _____ when I (spell) _____ a word.

2. We have to (place) _____ this torn, (used) _____ book.

3. Are you (able) _____ to (pay) _____ the money?

4. I was (sure) _____ whether she would (view) _____ the
   chapter before our test.

Name: _____

Spelling: Prefixes

Directions: Using the prefixes **un**, **re** and **mis**, make new words by adding them to the given words. Use each new word in a sentence.

1. cover

   _____

2. spell

   _____

3. understand

   _____

4. tie

   _____

5. write

   _____

6. adjust

   _____

7. turn

   _____

8. take

   _____

Directions: Find out what the prefixes **dis** and **in** mean. Then add each to one of the following words and write two sentences using two of the new words.

advantage	taste	direct	secure

_____

_____

Writing: Synonyms

A **synonym** is a word that means almost the same thing as another word.

Directions: Some words are used over and over again. Write three synonyms for each overused word below. You may want to look them up in a thesaurus, a book that lists synonyms for words.

1. good   _____   _____   _____

2. nice   _____   _____   _____

3. okay   _____   _____   _____

4. pretty   _____   _____   _____

5. little   _____   _____   _____

6. big   _____   _____   _____

Directions: Rewrite the paragraph below, replacing the underlined words with interesting synonyms. Add at least ten new words to the paragraph. Use your own paper if necessary.

One day in a store I saw a <u>nice</u> jacket. I wanted to buy it to replace my old jacket. I had worn my old jacket a <u>pretty</u> long time. It still looked <u>okay</u>, but I was tired of it. I didn't think my parents would buy me a new jacket, so I did something very unusual. I decided to earn some money and buy the jacket myself. My parents said that would be <u>okay</u>. I got a job cutting my neighbors' grass. When I was finished, they told me I did a <u>nice</u> job. I was pretty hot and tired, but I felt <u>good</u> about making some money by myself.

_____

_____

_____

_____

_____

_____

Name: _____

Writing: Exercising Your Imagination

Directions: Often people use the same words over and over to say that one thing is like another: as hot as fire, as cold as ice. Think of new ways to tell about things and write them below.

Example: to fly like a bird   <u>to fly like an eagle</u>

1. as blue as the sky   _____

2. as soft as a cloud   _____

3. as dark as night   _____

4. as hard as rocks   _____

5. as light as a feather   _____

6. to grow like a weed   _____

7. to swim like a fish   _____

8. as quiet as a mouse   _____

9. to run like the wind   _____

10. to sleep like a baby   _____

Now pick five of your new ways to tell about things and use them in sentences.

_____

_____

_____

_____

_____

Writing: Telling What's Happening

Use a simple verb or add **ing** to tell what is happening now, using **is** or **are**.

Examples: He **talks**.   He is **talking**.
They **taste** the food.   They **are tasting** the food.

Directions: Write two sentences for each verb below. Write the verb both ways. Remember, if a verb ends with **e**, drop the **e** before adding **ing**.

Example:

rewrite

1. The girl rewrites her spelling words.

2. She is rewriting her spelling words.

replace

_____

_____

repay

_____

_____

misspell

_____

_____

misuse

_____

_____

Name: _____

Writing: Telling What Already Happened

Add **ed** or **ing** to the verb to tell what has already happened, using **was** or **were**.

Example: She **talked**.   She **was talking**.
                They **hoped**.   They **were hoping**.

Directions: Write two sentences for each verb below. Write the verb both ways.

Example:

unfasten

1. He unfastened his dog's leash.

2. He was unfastening the dog's leash.

repeat

_____

_____

misplace

_____

_____

return

_____

_____

refuse

_____

_____

remain

_____

_____

Name:_____

Writing: Comparing and Contrasting

A **comparison** is a way to show the similarities and differences between two things. Another way to say this is "compare and contrast."

Directions: Practice comparing things by telling how books and movies are the same and how they are different.

1. First, make a list of the ways they are the same and a list of the ways they are different.
2. Then, use your ideas to write a paragraph about their likenesses and a paragraph about their differences. Begin both paragraphs with topic sentences. (Use more paper if needed.)
   Here is an example comparing dogs and cats:

Ways they are the same:
   both animals
   both kept as pets
   both small and furry

Ways they are different:
   cats take care of themselves
   dogs easier to teach tricks
   cats picky about their food

Topic sentences for two paragraphs:
   Dogs and cats are the same in many ways.
   (followed by supporting sentences giving details)

   Still, no one could mistake a dog for a cat because of all the ways they are different.
   (followed by supporting sentences)

Write lists comparing books and movies.

Ways they are the same:

_____

_____

Ways they are different:

_____

_____

Write two paragraphs on another sheet of paper, comparing and contrasting books and movies. Begin each paragraph with a topic sentence.

Name: _____

Writing: Comparing and Contrasting

One way to organize information for a "compare and contrast" essay is to use a Venn diagram. A **Venn diagram** is used to chart information that shows similarities and differences between two things.

Study the following example comparing apples and oranges:

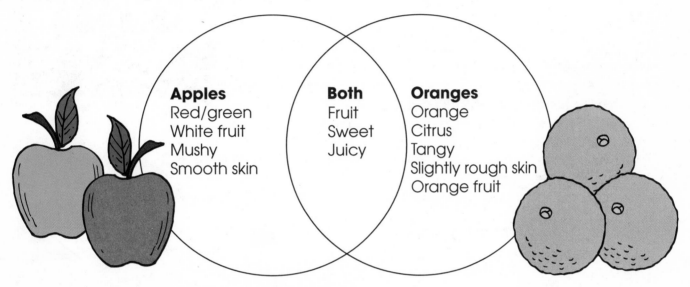

Apples
Red/green
White fruit
Mushy
Smooth skin

Both
Fruit
Sweet
Juicy

Oranges
Orange
Citrus
Tangy
Slightly rough skin
Orange fruit

In the first circle, all the apple details are given.
In the second circle, all the orange details are given.
Where the circles intersect, qualities similar to both fruits are given.

Directions: Think about two friends or relatives and write a "comparison" paper about them. To help organize your thoughts, complete the Venn diagram below. Then write a two-paragraph essay on another sheet of paper.

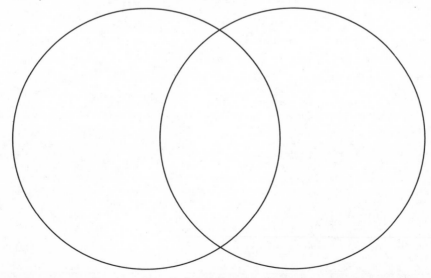

Name:_____

Review

Directions: Write several paragraphs that describe your bedroom.

Follow these steps:
1. Begin by writing all your ideas on another sheet of paper.
2. Choose the ideas you want to use and group them into paragraphs.
3. Write the ideas in sentences. Begin each paragraph with a topic sentence, followed with details in supporting sentences.
4. Use some words with prefixes, such as **misplace**, **unable**, **unsure**, **replace** and **refill**. Be sure to use synonyms for the words **good**, **pretty**, **nice**, **okay**, **big** and **little**. Be careful when using possessive forms.
5. Read your paragraphs aloud. Could someone draw a picture of your bedroom after reading your description?
6. Make any needed changes and rewrite your paragraphs below. Use more paper if needed.
7. Have someone read your description and see if he/she can draw a picture of your bedroom!

My Bedroom

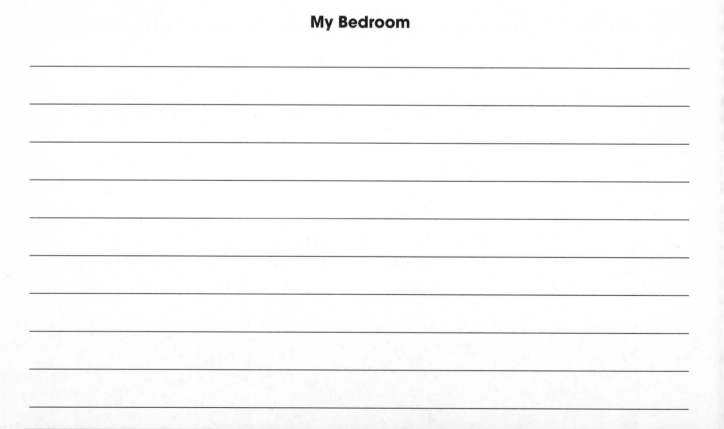

_____

_____

_____

_____

_____

_____

_____

_____

_____

_____

Name: _____

Spelling: Suffixes

A **suffix** is a syllable added to the end of a word that changes its meaning. Here are some suffixes: **ful** as in **beautiful**, **ment** as in **excitement** and **ion** as in **vacation**.

Often suffixes change the way a word is used. For example, a suffix can change a noun (**beauty**) to an adjective (**beautiful**) or a verb (**excite**) to a noun (**excitement**).

Directions: Add the suffixes to make new words:

protect	+	ion	=	_____
improve	+	ment	=	_____
cheer	+	ful	=	_____
disappoint	+	ment	=	_____
collect	+	ion	=	_____
thank	+	ful	=	_____
invent	+	ion	=	_____
help	+	ful	=	_____
play	+	ful	=	_____
state	+	ment	=	_____

Directions: Add **ful**, **ment** or **ion** to each word below.

1. The puppies are always so (play) _____.

2. Be (thank) _____ the children feel so (cheer) _____.

3. He was (help) _____ when I made my (collect) _____

_____.

4. These seatbelts are an (improve) _____ to the car's design.

5. They are made for your (protect) _____ in case of an accident.

6. Our team's loss was a (disappoint) _____.

7. He read a (state) _____ about the (invent) _____.

Name: _____

Spelling: Suffixes

Directions: Add a suffix to each word to make a new word. Then write the new word's meaning: **ion** and **ment** mean "state of being or outcome"; **ful** means "to be full of."

			Words	**Meaning**

rebell   + ion   = _____   _____

doubt   + ful   = _____   _____

pay   + ment   = _____   _____

commune + ion   = _____   _____

treat   + ment   = _____   _____

beauty   + ful   = _____   _____

react   + ion   = _____   _____

amuse   + ment   = _____   _____

thank   + ful   = _____   _____

select   + ion   = _____   _____

manage   + ment   = _____   _____

help   + ful   = _____   _____

Directions: Below are words with suffixes. Underline the root word and circle the suffix. The first one has been done for you.

1. <u>resent</u>(ment)

2. prayerful

3. objection

4. payment

5. sorrowful

6. invention

7. contentment

8. adjustment

9. devotion

10. cheerful

11. useful

12. pollution

Name: _____

Spelling: Prefixes and Suffixes

Directions: Use the prefixes and suffixes below to complete the exercises.

The prefix **pre** means "before." **Prepay** means "to pay before."
The prefix **dis** means "not." **Dismount** means "not mount."
The prefix **en** means "to cause or make happen." **Entrust** means "to trust."

The suffix **able** means "able to." **Likeable** means "able to like."
The suffix **less** means "without." **Painless** means "without pain."
The suffix **ness** means "a state of being." **Happiness** means "being happy."

prefix
+

base word
+

suffix

		Words	**Meanings**

1. pre   + game   = _____   _____

2. enjoy   + able   = _____   _____

3. dis   + trust   = _____   _____

4. en   + camp   = _____   _____

5. thought + less   = _____   _____

6. eager   + ness   = _____   _____

7. pre   + arrange   = _____   _____

8. dis   + content   = _____   _____

9. en   + able   = _____   _____

10. home   + less   = _____   _____

11. lovely   + ness   = _____   _____

12. laugh   + able   = _____   _____

Directions: Select four words from above—two with prefixes and two with suffixes. Use each one correctly in a sentence.

_____

_____

_____

_____

Name:_____

Writing: Putting Ideas Together

Directions: Combine each pair of sentences below, using conjunctions (**and**, **or**, **but**, **when**, **after**, **because**) and all the other ways you have learned.

1. This improvement will save lives. This improvement will also save money.

   _____

   _____

2. Mrs. Thompson was helpful when I had trouble with math. Mrs. Thompson is my teacher.

   _____

   _____ .

3. Mike was cheerful this morning. Penny was cheerful, too.

   _____

   _____

4. He started to read a statement. He did not finish it.

   _____

   _____

5. Our team lost. We tried to hide our disappointment.

   _____

   _____

6. We were outside looking for insects. We had to make a collection for science.

   _____

   _____

7. No one was hurt in the accident. We were thankful.

   _____

   _____

8. Is that your own invention? Is it someone else's idea?

   _____

Spelling: Counting Syllables

Directions: Use words from the box to answer the questions.

playful	protection	disappointment	cheerful	statement
invention	improvement	thankful	collection	helpful

1. Write each word from the box on the line that tells how many syllables it has.

   Two: _____ _____ _____ _____

   Three: _____ _____ _____ _____

   Four: _____

2. Write words from the box that are synonyms for the ones below. Use each word only once.

   discovery: _____   grateful: _____

   useful: _____   a repair: _____

   shelter: _____   joking: _____

   group: _____   happy: _____

   sentence: _____   defeat: _____

3. Unscramble the letters to spell words from the box.

   ttoonrpcei _____   llpfuay _____

   eeclfruh _____   tnhkuafl _____

   mmeetroipvn _____   eetttanms _____

   ppttnniidasmeo _____   oollccneit _____

   nnniivote _____   llhufpe _____

SPELLING 4

Writing: Facts and Opinions

A **fact** is information that can be proven true. An **opinion** is information that tells how someone feels or what he/she thinks about something or someone.

Directions: Write an **F** by the facts and an **O** by the opinions.

_____ 1. The scientist announced the invention on March 4, 1990.

_____ 2. This invention will save the human race.

_____ 3. The improvement to the building cost $300.

_____ 4. The building is much more comfortable now.

_____ 5. Bob's collection of baseball cards is the best at school.

_____ 6. He has 139 cards in his collection.

_____ 7. The police provided protection for the movie star.

_____ 8. Without their protection, he would have been hurt.

_____ 9. He looks more cheerful today than yesterday.

_____ 10. You should be thankful I'm your sister.

Write a fact about your school: _____

Write an opinion about your school: _____

Writing: Facts and Opinions

Directions: Write an **F** by the facts and an **O** by the opinions.

_____ 1. Jessie ate lunch at 12 noon.

_____ 2. Jessie thinks peanut butter is the best.

_____ 3. Wanda is the only girl on the football team.

_____ 4. I think football is a violent sport.

_____ 5. Seven people were injured on the football team last season.

_____ 6. Two of the football players weigh over 250 pounds!

_____ 7. No one should weigh 250 pounds!

_____ 8. I'm going to take that class over again.

_____ 9. I think I'm good at math.

_____ 10. According to this survey, math is the favorite subject of 25% of the students.

_____ 11. Miranda has two horses and three cats.

_____ 12. Miranda says riding horses at sunset is the only way to see a sunset.

_____ 13. Mr. Sims says Leroy is going to get the highest grade in the class.

_____ 14. He thought his grades weren't good enough.

_____ 15. At this school, we grade on the bell curve.

Write one fact and one opinion about your favorite school subject.

Fact: _____

Opinion: _____

Name: _____

Spelling: Finding Mistakes

Directions: Circle all the spelling mistakes in the paragraph below. (Some are from earlier lessons.) Then write each word correctly on the lines under the story.

My frendship with Justin means a lot to me. When I heard he was going to move a long distanse away, all I felt was disapointment. "Just be thankfull he was your friend all those years," my sister said. She was trying to be helpfull, but I was in pane!

Justin and I got to be friends in grad one, when we shared our colections of little trucks. I remember that Justin klaimed I broke his firetruck. It was an acident, but he acused me of doing it on purpose! I had to replase his dumb truck! Another time, we made an invenshun. It was a new alfabet so we could write secret notes to each other. Then I missplaced our only copy. Boy, was Justin mad! I told him it was no big deel!

I'll try to look cheerful when he leaves, but I know my stomack will hurt. I'll even miss all his frekles and the way he always sneeses around my cat. At least I can call him on the fone. I might even right him a letter . . . Nah!

_____   _____   _____

_____   _____   _____

_____   _____   _____

_____   _____   _____

_____   _____   _____

_____   _____   _____

Name: _____

Review

Directions: Write at least two paragraphs below. First, write facts about your favorite TV show. What is it called and when is it on? Who are some of the actors? Are they all part of one family? Where do they live? Do they have jobs?

Then write your opinions about the show. What makes it your favorite? Why do you think other people should watch it? Follow these steps:

1. Write your ideas for both paragraphs on another sheet of paper.
2. Choose the ideas you want to use. Write the facts in one paragraph and the opinions in the other. Then put the ideas in order in each paragraph and write them in sentences.
3. Try to work in some of the words with suffixes, like **cheerful**, **protection** and **disappointment**. Combine some of your shorter sentences with joining words.
4. Read your paragraphs aloud to see if they're clear. Make any needed changes.
5. Rewrite the paragraphs below. Use more paper if needed.
6. Give your paper to someone else. Does he/she like the same show you do?

Facts about my favorite TV show:

_____

_____

_____

_____

My opinions about the show:

_____

_____

_____

_____

_____

Name: _____

SPELLING 4

Writing: All About Me

Directions: Follow the instructions to write an essay about yourself.

Think about your life so far. When were you born? When did you learn to walk, talk and run? What is your family like? Do you have any brothers or sisters or pets? Where do you live? What is your house like? What has school been like for you? Do you like school? What is your favorite grade or subject? Do you play sports? Do you have hobbies?

Use the following "cluster of ideas" chart to organize your thoughts. Number your clusters in the order they will appear in the essay. Add more clusters if needed. Write your essay on another sheet of paper, edit it using the marks on page 105 and write your final draft on page 106.

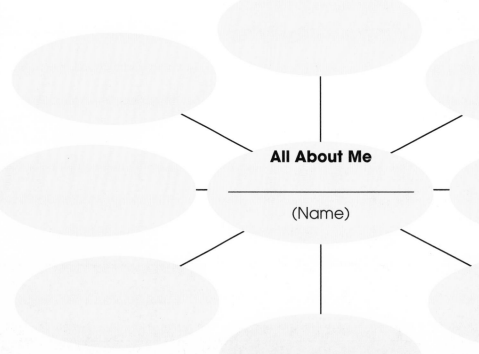

All About Me

_____

(Name)

Writing: Editing

Every author must edit his/her writing before making a final draft. Sometimes, even the best authors miss mistakes in their writing, and an editor will check their work much like a parent or teacher checks yours. The following editing marks are used by both editors and teachers.

Directions: Using the editing marks below, go back and edit the essay you wrote about yourself. When you have made the proper corrections, reread your essay, or have a parent or friend read it for you. Can you find any more mistakes? If so, edit your work again. When your final draft is ready, copy it on to page 106. Draw a picture to go with your essay when you are finished.

≡	capitalize letter	jenna was always late to school.
∧	insert something	Jenna was ^{always} late to school.
∧	add comma	Jenna, a fourth-grade student, was always late to school.
⊙	add period	Jenna was always late to school⊙
/	make lower-case	Jenna was always late to school.
——	correct spelling	Jenna was ~~awlays~~ always late to school.
∿	transpose	Jenna was late always to school.
∨ ∨	insert quotation marks	Jenna, she said, "you must stop being late to school."
¶	start new paragraph	Jenna was always late to school. She tried so hard to be on time, but she couldn't manage her time. ¶ One day, as Jenna was getting ready for school, she spilled orange juice all over the front of her new shirt. She would be late again!

Name: _____

Writing: All About Me

Glossary

Action Verb: Tells the action of a sentence.

Adjective: A word that tells more about or describes a noun, such as **happy** child or **cold** day.

Adverb: A word that describes a verb. It tells how, when or where action takes place.

Apostrophe: A punctuation mark that shows possession (**Kim's** hat) or takes the place of missing letters in a word (**isn't**).

Cause: The reason that something happens.

Cinquain: A five-line poem following a specific format.

Command: A sentence that tells someone to do something.

Common Noun: Names a "general" person, place or thing.

Comparison: A way to show the similarities and differences between two things.

Conjunctions (Joining Words): Words that join sentences or combine ideas, such as **and**, **but**, **or**, **because**, **when**, **after**, and so on.

Consonants: All the letters except **a**, **e**, **i**, **o**, **u** and sometimes **y**.

Effect: Something that happens as the result of a cause.

Exclamation: A sentence that shows strong feeling or excitement.

Fact: Information that can be proven true.

Future-Tense Verb: Tells what will happen in the future.

Helping Verb: Used with an action verb to "help" the action of a sentence.

Joining Words (Conjunctions): Words that join sentences or combine ideas, such as **and**, **but**, **or**, **because**, **when**, **after**, and so on.

Linking Verb: Joins the subject and predicate of a sentence.

Noun: A word that names a person, place or thing.

Opinion: Information that tells how someone feels or what he/she thinks about something or someone.

Paragraph: A group of sentences that tells about one main idea.

Past-Tense Verb: Tells about action that has already happened.

Plural: A word that refers to more than one thing, such as **hats** or **mittens**.

Possessive Noun: A noun that shows something belongs to the noun, such as **Jill's** book.

Predicate: The part of a sentence that tells what the subject is doing.

Prefix: A syllable added to the beginning of a word that changes its meaning.

Present-Tense Verb: Tells what is happening now.

Proper Noun: Names a "specific" person, place or thing.

Question: A sentence that asks for a specific piece of information.

Sentence: A group of words that expresses a complete thought; it must have a noun (subject) and a verb.

Singular: A word that refers to only one thing, such as **hat** or **mitten**.

Statement: A sentence that tells some kind of information.

Story Map: A diagram that helps to organize thoughts in a logical sequence.

Subject: Part of a sentence that tells who or what the sentence is about.

Suffix: A syllable added to the end of a word that changes its meaning.

Supporting Sentence: A sentence that provides details about the topic sentence of a paragraph.

Syllable: A word—or part of a word—with only one vowel sound.

Synonym: A word that means almost the same thing as another word.

Topic Sentence: The sentence that tells the main idea of a paragraph.

Venn Diagram: A diagram used to chart information that shows similarities and differences between two things.

Verb: The action word in a sentence; the word that tells what something does or that something exists.

Vowels: The letters **a**, **e**, **i**, **o**, **u** and sometimes **y**.

Answer Key

Spelling: Short Vowels

Vowels are the letters a, e, i, o, u and sometimes y. There are five short vowels: **ă** as in **a**pple, **ĕ** as in **e**gg and br**ea**th, **ĭ** as in s**i**ck, **ŏ** as in t**o**p and **ŭ** as in **u**p.

Directions: Complete the exercises using words from the box.

| blend | insist | health | pump | crop |
| fact | pinch | pond | hatch | plug |

1. Write each word under its vowel sound.

ă	ĕ	ĭ	ŏ	ŭ
fact	blend	insist	pond	pump
hatch	health	pinch	crop	plug

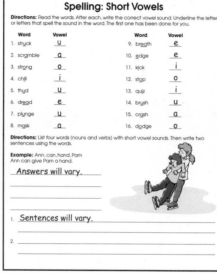
UP

2. Complete these sentences, using a word with the vowel sound given. Use each word from the box only once.

Here's an interesting (ă) __fact__ about your (ĕ) __health__.

Henry was very pleased with his corn (ŏ) __crop__

The boys enjoyed fishing in the (ŏ) __pond__.

They (ĭ) __insist__ on watching the egg (ă) __hatch__

(ĕ) __Blend__ in a (ĭ) __pinch__ of salt.

The farmer had to (ŭ) __pump__ water from the lake for his cows to drink.

Did you put the (ŭ) __plug__ in the bathtub this time?

3

Spelling: Short Vowels

Directions: Read the words. After each, write the correct vowel sound. Underline the letter or letters that spell the sound in the word. The first one has been done for you.

	Word	Vowel		Word	Vowel
1.	str**u**ck	u	9.	br**ea**th	e
2.	scr**a**mble	a	10.	**e**dge	e
3.	str**o**ng	o	11.	k**i**ck	i
4.	ch**i**ll	i	12.	st**o**p	o
5.	th**u**d	u	13.	qu**i**z	i
6.	dr**ea**d	e	14.	br**u**sh	u
7.	pl**u**nge	u	15.	cr**a**sh	a
8.	m**a**sk	a	16.	d**o**dge	o

Directions: List four words (nouns and verbs) with short vowel sounds. Then write two sentences using the words.

Example: Ann, can, hand, Pam
Ann can give Pam a hand.

__Answers will vary.__
_____
_____

1. __Sentences will vary.__ _____
_____

2. _____
_____

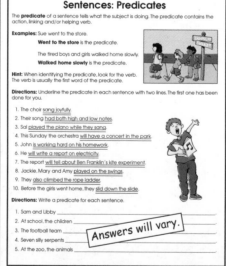

4

Writing: Sentences

A **sentence** is a group of words that expresses a complete thought.

Directions: Write **S** by each group of words that is a sentence and **NS** by those that are not a complete sentence.

Examples:

__NS__ A pinch of salt in the soup.

__S__ Grandmother was fond of her flower garden.

__S__ 1. Tigers blend in with their surroundings.

__NS__ 2. Our crop of vegetables for this summer.

__S__ 3. Don't forget to put the plug in the sink.

__NS__ 4. Usually older people in good health.

__NS__ 5. Fond of lying in the sun for hours.

__S__ 6. Will ducks hatch a swan egg?

__S__ 7. I hope he won't insist on coming with us.

__S__ 8. Regular exercise will pump up your muscles.

__NS__ 9. A fact printed in all the newspapers.

__S__ 10. Did you pinch the baby?

__S__ 11. Plug the hole with your finger.

__NS__ 12. A new teacher today in health class.

__S__ 13. I insist on giving you some of my candy.

__NS__ 14. A blend of peanut butter and honey.

__NS__ 15. As many facts as possible in your report.

5

Sentences: Subjects

The **subject** of a sentence tells you who or what the sentence is about. A subject is either a common or proper noun.

Examples: Sue went to the store.

Sue is the subject of the sentence.

The tired boys and girls walked home slowly.

The tired boys and girls is the subject of the sentence.

Directions: Underline the subject of each sentence. The first one has been done for you.

1. The birthday cake was pink and white.
2. Anthony celebrated his fourth birthday.
3. The tower of building blocks fell over.
4. On Saturday, our family will go to a movie.
5. The busy editor was writing sentences.
6. Seven children painted pictures.
7. Two happy dolphins played cheerfully on the surf.
8. A sand crab buried itself in the dunes.
9. Blue waves ran peacefully ashore.
10. Sleepily, she went to bed.

Directions: Write a subject for each sentence.

1. __Chocolate-chip ice cream__ was melting in the
2. _____ ran do
3. _____
4. _____
5. _____ her a beautiful dress.
6. _____ hopped, skipped and jumped all the way home.
7. _____ wrote a long letter.
8. _____ moved to Paris, France.

__Answers will vary.__

6

Sentences: Predicates

The **predicate** of a sentence tells what the subject is doing. The predicate contains the action, linking and/or helping verb.

Examples: Sue went to the store.

Went to the store is the predicate.

The tired boys and girls walked home slowly.

Walked home slowly is the predicate.

Hint: When identifying the predicate, look for the verb. The verb is usually the first word of the predicate.

Directions: Underline the predicate in each sentence with two lines. The first one has been done for you.

1. The choir sang joyfully.
2. Their song had both high and low notes.
3. Sal played the piano while they sang.
4. This Sunday the orchestra will have a concert in the park.
5. John is working hard on his homework.
6. He will write a report on electricity.
7. The report will tell about Ben Franklin's kite experiment.
8. Jackie, Mary and Amy played on the swings.
9. They also climbed the rope ladder.
10. Before the girls went home, they slid down the slide.

Directions: Write a predicate for each sentence.

1. Sam and Libby _____
2. At school, the children _____
3. The football team _____
4. Seven silly serpents _____
5. At the zoo, the animals _____

__Answers will vary.__

7

Writing: Subjects and Predicates

Directions: Draw a line to connect the subjects with the correct predicates to make complete sentences.

Subjects	Predicates
1. The busy mall	went to sleep in her stroller.
2. The restaurants	bought two new dresses.
3. The children	was full of shoppers.
4. Mom	served delicious food.
5. The baby	purchased new sneakers for school.

SUBJECT & PREDICATE

Directions: Read the following sentences. Underline the subject once and the predicate twice. The first one has been done for you.

1. The busy editor wrote a page about subjects and predicates.
2. She was hopeful the children would understand sentences.
3. The school children completed their pages quickly.
4. When their work was finished, they went outside.
5. The teacher watched the boys play ball.
6. The girls swung on the swings and climbed the monkey bars.
7. Kim, Luke, Jill and Matt enjoyed their time outdoors.
8. They were refreshed when they came inside.
9. The children ran outside after the storm.
10. Fall had always been her favorite time of year.

8

Spelling: Listening for Vowels

Directions: Circle the word in each row with the same vowel sound as the first word. The first one has been done for you.

blend	twig	brand	(fed)	bleed
fact	first	(bad)	shell	bead
plug	card	steal	(stuff)	pian
pinch	(kiss)	reach	ripe	come
health	dear	bath	top	(head)
crop	hope	(stock)	drip	strap

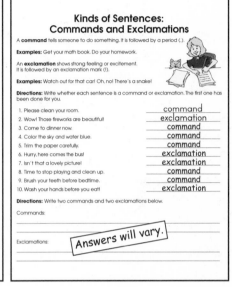

Directions: Write the words from the box that answer the questions.

| blend | insist | health | pump | crop | fact | pinch | fond | hatch | plug |

1. Which two words have the same vowel as the first vowel in **bundle**?

   pump , plug

2. Which two words have the same vowel as the first vowel in **bottle**?

   crop , fond

3. Which two words have the same vowel as the first vowel in **wilderness**?

   insist , pinch

4. Which two words have the same vowel as the first vowel in **manner**?

   fact , hatch

5. Which two words have the same vowel as the first vowel in **measure**?

   blend , health

9

Kinds of Sentences: Statements and Questions

A **statement** tells some kind of information. It is followed by a period (.).

Examples: It is a rainy day. We are going to the beach next summer.

A **question** asks for a specific piece of information. It is followed by a question mark (?).

Examples: What is the weather like today? When are you going to the beach?

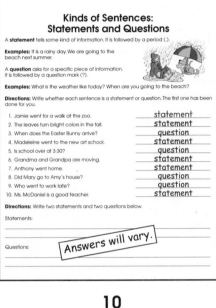

Directions: Write whether each sentence is a statement or question. The first one has been done for you.

1. Jamie went for a walk at the zoo. statement
2. The leaves turn bright colors in the fall. statement
3. When does the Easter Bunny arrive? question
4. Madeleine went to the new art school. statement
5. Is school over at 3:30? question
6. Grandma and Grandpa are moving. statement
7. Anthony went home. statement
8. Did Mary go to Amy's house? question
9. Who went to work late? question
10. Ms. McDaniel is a good teacher. statement

Directions: Write two statements and two questions below.

Statements:

Questions: Answers will vary.

10

Kinds of Sentences: Commands and Exclamations

A **command** tells someone to do something. It is followed by a period (.).

Examples: Get your math book. Do your homework.

An **exclamation** shows strong feeling or excitement. It is followed by an exclamation mark (!).

Examples: Watch out for that car! Oh, no! There's a snake!

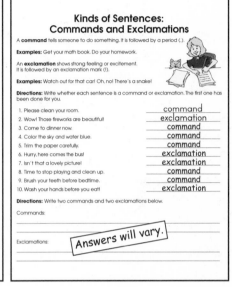

Directions: Write whether each sentence is a command or exclamation. The first one has been done for you.

1. Please clean your room. command
2. Wow! Those fireworks are beautiful! exclamation
3. Come to dinner now. command
4. Color the sky and water blue. command
5. Trim the paper carefully. command
6. Hurry, here comes the bus! exclamation
7. Isn't that a lovely picture! exclamation
8. Time to stop playing and clean up. command
9. Brush your teeth before bedtime. command
10. Wash your hands before you eat! exclamation

Directions: Write two commands and two exclamations below.

Commands:

Exclamations: Answers will vary.

11

Writing: Four Kinds of Sentences

Directions: Write **S** for statement, **Q** for question, **C** for command or **E** for exclamation. End each sentence with a period, question mark or exclamation mark.

Example: _E_ You better watch out!

_S_ 1. My little brother insists on coming with us .

_C_ 2. Tell him movies are bad for his health .

_S_ 3. He says he's fond of movies .

_Q_ 4. Does he know there are monsters in this movie ?

_S_ 5. He says he needs facts for his science report .

_S_ 6. He's writing about something that hatched from an old egg .

_Q_ 7. Couldn't he just go to the library ?

_Q_ 8. Could we dress him like us so he'll blend in ?

_E or Q_ 9. Are you kidding ! or ?

_Q_ 10. Would he sit by himself at the movie ?

_S or E_ 11. That would be too dangerous . or !

_S_ 12. Mom said she'd give us money for candy if we took him with us .

_Q_ 13. Why didn't you say that earlier ?

_C or E_ 14. Get your brother and let's go . or !

12

Spelling: Making New Words

Directions: Use words from the box to answer the questions.

blend	fond
fact	pump
insist	hatch
pinch	crop
health	plug

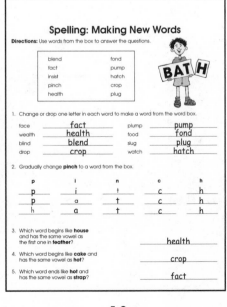

1. Change or drop one letter in each word to make a word from the word box.

face	fact	plump	pump
wealth	health	food	fond
blind	blend	slug	plug
drop	crop	watch	hatch

2. Gradually change **pinch** to a word from the box.

p	i	n	c	h
p	i	t	c	h
p	a	t	c	h
h	a	t	c	h

3. Which word begins like **house** and has the same vowel as the first one in **feather**? health

4. Which word begins like **cake** and has the same vowel as **hot**? crop

5. Which word ends like **hot** and has the same vowel as **strap**? fact

13

Spelling: Word Ladders

Word ladders are a fun way of creating new words by changing one letter/sound in the original word.

Example: By changing one letter with each step, the word **hat** is changed to **bed**.

hat
bat
bet
bed

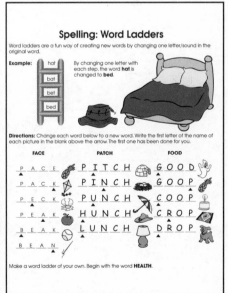

Directions: Change each word below to a new word. Write the first letter of the name of each picture in the blank above the arrow. The first one has been done for you.

FACE	PATCH	FOOD
P A C E	P I T C H	G O O D
P A C K	P I N C H	G O O P
P E C K	P U N C H	C O O P
P E A K	H U N C H	C R O P
B E A K	L U N C H	D R O P
B E A N		

Make a word ladder of your own. Begin with the word **HEALTH**.

14

Writing: Four Kinds of Sentences

Directions: For each pair of words, write two kinds of sentences (any combination of question, command, statement or exclamation). Use one or both words in each sentence. Name each kind of sentence you wrote.

Example: pump   crop

Question: What kind of crops did you plant?

Command: Pump the water as fast as you can.

1. pinch   health

_____ : _____

_____ : _____

2. fond   fact

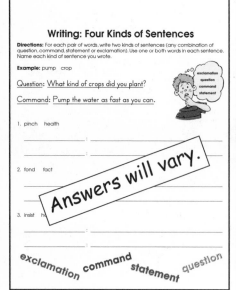

Answers will vary.

3. insist   ha...

_____

_____

exclamation   command   statement   question

15

Writing: Verbs

Verbs are the action words in a sentence. There are three kinds of verbs: action verbs, linking verbs and helping verbs.

An **action verb** tells the action of a sentence.

Examples: run, hop, skip, sleep, jump, talk, snore
Michael **ran** to the store. **Ran** is the action verb.

A **linking verb** joins the subject and predicate of a sentence.

Examples: am, is, are, was, were
Michael **was** at the store. **Was** is the linking verb.

A **helping verb** is used with an action verb to "help" the action of the sentence.

Examples: am, is, are, was, were
Matthew **was** helping Michael. **Was** helps the action verb **helping**.

Directions: Read the following sentences. Underline the verbs. Above each, write **A** for action verb, **L** for linking verb and **H** for helping verb. The first one has been done for you.

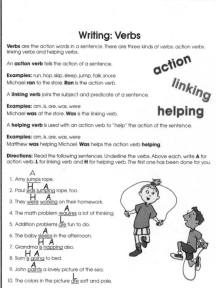

action   linking   helping

1. Amy jumps rope. (A)
2. Paul was jumping rope, too. (H A)
3. They were working on their homework. (H A)
4. The math problem requires a lot of thinking. (A)
5. Addition problems are fun to do. (A)
6. The baby sleeps in the afternoon. (A)
7. Grandma is napping also. (H A)
8. Sam is going to bed. (H A)
9. John paints a lovely picture of the sea. (A)
10. The colors in the picture are soft and pale. (L)

16

Writing: Verb Tense

Not only do verbs tell the action of a sentence but they also tell when the action takes place. This is called the **verb tense**. There are three verb tenses: past, present and future tense.

Present-tense verbs tell what is happening now.

Example: Jane **spells** words with long vowel sounds.

Past-tense verbs tell about action that has already happened. Past-tense verbs are usually formed by adding **ed** to the verb.

Example: stay — stayed
John **stayed** home yesterday.

Past-tense verbs can also be made by adding helping verbs **was** or **were** before the verb and adding **ing** to the verb.

Example: talk — was talking
Sally **was talking** to her mom.

Future-tense verbs tell what will happen in the future. Future-tense verbs are made by putting the word **will** before the verb.

Example: paint — will paint
Susie and Sherry **will paint** the house.

Directions: Read the following verbs. Write whether the verb tense is past, present or future.

Verb	Tense	Verb	Tense
1. watches	present	8. writes	present
2. wanted	past	9. vaulted	past
3. will eat	future	10. were sleeping	past
4. was squawking	past	11. will sing	future
5. yawns	present	12. is speaking	present
6. crawled	past	13. will cook	future
7. will hunt	future	14. likes	present

17

Writing: Verb Tense

Directions: Read the following sentences. Underline the verbs. Above each, write whether it is past, present or future tense.

1. The crowd was booing the referee. (past)
2. Sally will compete on the balance beam. (future)
3. Matt marches with the band. (present)
4. Nick is marching, too. (present)
5. The geese swooped down to the pond. (past)
6. Dad will fly home tomorrow. (future)
7. They were looking for a new book. (past)
8. Presently, they are going to the garden. (present)
9. The children will pick the ripe vegetables. (future)
10. Grandmother canned the green beans. (past)

past   future   present

Directions: Write six sentences of your own using the correct verb tense.

Past tense:

Sentences will vary.

Present tense:

Future tense:

18

Writing: Present-Tense Verbs

Directions: Write two sentences for each verb below. Tell about something that is happening now and write the verb as both simple present tense and present tense with a helping verb.

Example: run
Mia runs to the store.   Mia is running to the store.

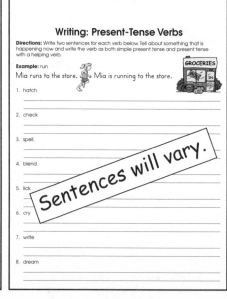

1. hatch

2. check

3. spell

4. blend

Sentences will vary.

5. lick

6. cry

7. write

8. dream

19

Review

Directions: Read the sentence below. Circle all five short vowels. (Two words in the sentence do not have short vowels.)

Pat bent to pick up the dog.

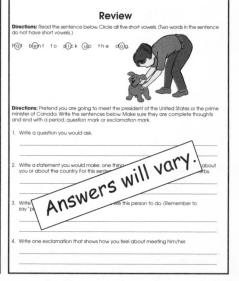

Directions: Pretend you are going to meet the president of the United States or the prime minister of Canada. Write the sentences below. Make sure they are complete thoughts and end with a period, question mark or exclamation mark.

1. Write a question you would ask.

2. Write a statement you would make: one thing ... about you or about the country. For this sente... ...rbs.

3. Write ... ...e this person to do. (Remember to say "p...

Answers will vary.

4. Write one exclamation that shows how you feel about meeting him/her.

20

Spelling: Long e and a (21)

Long ē can be spelled **ea** as in **real** or **ee** as in **deer**. Long ā can be spelled **a** as in **apron**, **ai** as in **pail**, **ay** as in **pay** or **a-e** as in **lake**.

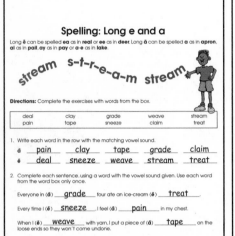

stream s-t-r-e-a-m stream

Directions: Complete the exercises with words from the box.

| deal | clay | grade | weave | stream |
| pain | tape | sneeze | claim | treat |

1. Write each word in the row with the matching vowel sound.

ā **pain**   **clay**   **tape**   **grade**   **claim**
ē **deal**   **sneeze**   **weave**   **stream**   **treat**

2. Complete each sentence, using a word with the vowel sound given. Use each word from the word box only once.

Everyone in (ā) **grade** four ate an ice-cream (ē) **treat**.

Every time I (ē) **sneeze**, I feel (ā) **pain** in my chest.

When I (ē) **weave** with yarn, I put a piece of (ā) **tape** on the loose ends so they won't come undone.

You (ā) **claim** you got a good (ē) **deal** on your new bike, but I still think you paid too much.

We camped beside a (ē) **stream**.

We forgot to wrap up our (ā) **clay** and it dried out.

21

Spelling: Long e and a (22)

When a vowel is long, it sounds the same as its letter name.

Examples: Long ē as in **treat, eel, complete.**
Long ā as in **ape, trail, say, apron.**

Directions: Read the words. After each word, write the correct vowel sound. Underline the letter or letters that spell the sound in the word. The first one has been done for you.

Word	Vowel		Word	Vowel
1. sp<u>ee</u>ch	e		9. pl<u>a</u>te	a
2. gr<u>ai</u>n	a		10. br<u>ee</u>ze	e
3. d<u>ea</u>l	e		11. wh<u>a</u>le	a
4. b<u>a</u>ste	a		12. cl<u>ay</u>	a
5. t<u>ea</u>ch	e		13. v<u>ea</u>l	e
6. w<u>ai</u>ting	a		14. <u>a</u>pron	a
7. cl<u>ea</u>ning	e		15. r<u>ai</u>ning	a
8. cr<u>a</u>ne	a		16. fr<u>ee</u>zer	e

Directions: Choose one long vowel sound. On another sheet of paper, list six words (nouns and verbs) that have that sound. Below, write two sentences using the words.

Example: freeze, teaches, breeze, speech, keep, Eve

Eve teaches speech in the breeze.

Sentences will vary.

22

Spelling: Vowel Sounds (23)

Directions: Follow the instructions below.

1. Circle the word in each row with the same vowel sound as the first word. The first one has been done for you.

deal	pail	church	(greet)	stove
pain	free	(frame)	twice	whole
weave	grape	stripe	(least)	thrill
grade	teach	(case)	joke	leave
treat	(greed)	throw	tent	truck

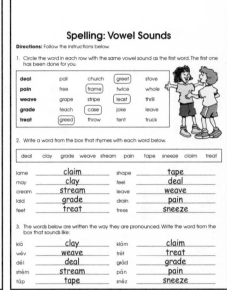

2. Write a word from the box that rhymes with each word below.

| deal | clay | grade | weave | stream | pain | tape | sneeze | claim | treat |

lame **claim**   shape **tape**
may   **clay**   feel   **deal**
cream **stream**   leave **weave**
laid **grade**   drain **pain**
feet **treat**   trees **sneeze**

3. The words below are written the way they are pronounced. Write the word from the box that sounds like:

klā **clay**   klām **claim**
wēv **weave**   trēt **treat**
dēl **deal**   grād **grade**
strēm **stream**   pān **pain**
tāp **tape**   snēz **sneeze**

23

Writing: Nouns (24)

A **noun** names a person, place or thing.

Examples: Persons — boy, girl, Mom, Dad
Places — park, pool, house, office
Things — bike, swing, desk, book

person place thing

Directions: Read the following sentences. Underline the nouns. The first one has been done for you.

1. The <u>girl</u> went to <u>school</u>.
2. <u>Grandma</u> and <u>Grandpa</u> will visit us soon.
3. The <u>bike</u> is in the <u>garage</u>.
4. <u>Dad</u> went to his <u>office</u>.
5. <u>Mom</u> is at her <u>desk</u> in the <u>den</u>.
6. <u>John</u>'s <u>house</u> is near the <u>park</u>.
7. Her <u>brothers</u> are at <u>school</u>.
8. We took the <u>books</u> to the <u>library</u>.

Words underlined in red can be used as both a noun and a verb.

Directions: Read the following words. Underline the nouns. Then categorize the nouns on another sheet of paper into groups of people, places and things.

tree	Mrs. Smith	Dad	cards	Grandma	skip	sell
house	car	truck	Mom	office	grass	sign
boy	run	Sam	stove	greet	grade	school
girl	camp	jump	weave	free	driver	room
salesperson	sad	teach	treat	stripe	paint	Jane
clay	man	leave	happy	play	desk	tape
watch	lives	painter	brother	rain	window	hop

24

Writing: Common and Proper Nouns (25)

Common nouns name general people, places and things.

Examples: boy, girl, cat, dog, park, city, building

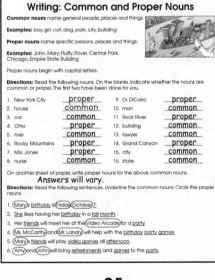

Proper nouns name specific persons, places and things.

Examples: John, Mary, Fluffy, Rover, Central Park, Chicago, Empire State Building

Proper nouns begin with capital letters.

Directions: Read the following nouns. On the blanks, indicate whether the nouns are common or proper. The first two have been done for you.

1. New York City	proper	9. Dr. DiCarlo	proper
2. house	common	10. man	common
3. car	common	11. Rock River	proper
4. Ohio	proper	12. building	common
5. river	common	13. lawyer	common
6. Rocky Mountains	proper	14. Grand Canyon	proper
7. Mrs. Jones	proper	15. city	common
8. nurse	common	16. state	common

On another sheet of paper, write proper nouns for the above common nouns.
Answers will vary.

Directions: Read the following sentences. Underline the common nouns. Circle the proper nouns.

1. (Mary)'s <u>birthday</u> is (Friday)(October) 7.
2. <u>She</u> likes having her <u>birthday</u> in a <u>fall</u> <u>month</u>.
3. Her <u>friends</u> will meet her at the (Video Arcade) for a <u>party</u>.
4. (Ms. McCarthy) and (Mr. Landry) will help with the <u>birthday</u> <u>party</u> <u>games</u>.
5. (Mary)'s <u>friends</u> will play <u>video games</u> all <u>afternoon</u>.
6. (Amy) and (John) will bring <u>refreshments</u> and <u>games</u> to the <u>party</u>.

25

Writing: Nouns or Verbs? (26)

Directions: Write one of the words from the box in each sentence pair. Write **N** over the word if it is used as a noun and **V** if it is used as a verb. You may need to add **s, es, ing** or **ed** to the verbs.

Example: The girl **sneezes**. Her **sneeze** scares the dog.

sneeze	tape
claim	treat
grade	stream
date	deal

1. I (V) **sneeze** around flowers. My (N) **sneeze** is louder than your (N) **sneeze**.
2. Let's go buy a (N) **treat** at the store. Today, I will (V) **treat** you to a candy bar.
3. Sometimes we (V) **grade** our own papers. I always get a higher (N) **grade** than Josh.
4. The rain (V) **streamed** down the window. The (N) **streamed** behind our house is overflowing.
5. Please (V) **tape** that TV show for me. I will watch the (N) **tape** when I come home.
6. A boy in my class (V) **claims** I took his candy bar. I know his (N) **claim** is wrong.
7. My brother has a (N) **date** tonight. He (V) **dates** the girl who lives next door.
8. Please (V) **deal** the cards. While we play, I'll tell you about the (N) **deal** I made with my sister.

26

Writing: Using Fewer Words

Writing can be more interesting when fewer words are used. Combining sentences is easy when the subjects are the same. Notice how the comma is used.

Example: Sally woke up. Sally ate breakfast. Sally brushed her teeth.

Sally woke up, ate breakfast and brushed her teeth.

Combining sentences with more than one subject is a little more complicated. Notice how commas are used to "set off" information.

Examples: Jane went to the store. Jane is Sally's sister.

Jane went to the store with Sally, her sister.

Eddie likes to play with cars. Eddie is my younger brother.

Eddie, my younger brother, likes to play with cars.

Directions: Write each pair of sentences as one sentence.

1. Jerry played soccer after school. He played with his best friend, Tom.
   Jerry played soccer after school with his best friend, Tom.
2. Spot likes to chase cats. Spot is my dog.
   Spot, my dog, likes to chase cats.
3. Lori and Janice both love ice cream. Janice is Lori's cousin.
   Lori and Janice, Lori's cousin, both like ice cream.
4. Jayna is my cousin. Jayna helped me move into my new apartment.
   Jayne, my cousin, helped me move into my new apartment.
5. Romeo is a big tomcat. Romeo loves to hunt mice.
   Romeo, a big tomcat, loves to hunt mice.

27

Writing: Using Fewer Words

Directions: Write each pair of sentences as one sentence.

Example: After school, Jerry ate some chocolate ice cream. It's his favorite treat.

Jerry ate his favorite treat, chocolate ice cream, after school.

Answers may include:

1. Benny keeps sneezing. Benny is my brother.
   My brother Benny keeps sneezing.
2. Kelly was dealing the cards. Kelly is my cousin.
   My cousin Kelly was dealing the cards.
3. Chris is in tenth grade. Chris is my baby-sitter.
   Chris, my baby-sitter, is in tenth grade.
4. Anna has a pain in her hand. Anna is my neighbor.
   My neighbor Anna has a pain in her hand.
5. I have two tapes of the Lipsticks. The Lipsticks are my favorite band.
   I have two tapes of the Lipsticks, my favorite band.
6. Jenny likes to play in the stream. Jenny is my sister.
   My sister Jenny likes to play in the stream.
7. Rachel brought me a treat. Rachel is my good friend.
   Rachel, my good friend, brought me a treat.
8. Judy Blume wrote this book. She is a very popular author.
   Judy Blume, a very popular author, wrote this book.
9. Mr. Thomas gave me this clay. Mr. Thomas is my teacher.
   Mr. Thomas, my teacher, gave me this clay.
10. I'm going to weave a rug in blue and white. Those are the colors in my bedroom.
    I'm going to weave a rug in blue and white, my bedroom colors.

28

Writing: Past-Tense Verbs

To write about something that already happened, you can add **ed** to the verb.

Example: Yesterday, we **talked**.

You can also use **was** and **were** and add **ing** to the verb.

Example: Yesterday, we **were talking**.
When a verb ends with **e**, you usually drop the **e** before adding **ing**.

Examples: grade — was grading   weave — were weaving
tape — was taping sneeze — were sneezing

Directions: Write two sentences for each verb below. Tell about something that has already happened and write the verb both ways.
(Watch the spelling of the verbs that end with **e**.)

Example: stream

The rain streamed down the window.
The rain was streaming down the window.

1. grade

2. tape

3. weave

4. sneeze

Sentences will vary.

29

Writing: Putting Ideas Together

Directions: Write each pair of sentences as one sentence.

Example: Jim will deal the cards one at a time. Jim will give four cards to everyone.

Jim will deal the cards one at a time and give four cards to everyone.

1. Amy won the contest.   Amy claimed the prize.
   Amy won the contest and claimed the prize.
2. We need to find the scissors.   We need to buy some tape.
   We need to find the scissors and buy some tape.
3. The stream runs through the woods.   The stream empties into the East River.
   The stream runs through the woods and empties into the river.
4. Katie tripped on the steps.   Katie has a pain in her left foot.
   Katie tripped on the steps and has a pain in her left foot.
5. Grandpa took me to the store.   Grandpa bought me a treat.
   Grandpa took me to the store and bought me a treat.
6. Charity ran 2 miles.   She walked 1 mile to cool down afterwards.
   Charity ran 2 miles and walked 1 mile to cool down afterwards.

30

Spelling: Making New Words

Directions: Unscramble these letters to spell the ā and ē words you have been practicing. If you need help with spelling, look at the box on page 23. The first one has been done for you.

ay + lc = clay   ee + zsne = sneeze
ea + mtrs = stream   a-e + pt = tape
ea + vew = weave   a-e + drg = grade
ea + rtt = treat   ai + np = pain
ea + ld = lead   ai + mlc = claim

Directions: Circle the spelling mistakes and write the words correctly. The first one has been done for you.

1. We made statues out of cley.   clay
2. Do you ever fish in that streem?   stream
3. Jason sneesed really loudly in class.   sneezed
4. Running gives me a pane in my side.   pain
5. We are tapeing the show for you.   taping
6. She klaims she won, but I came in first.   claims
7. Would you share your treet with me?   treat
8. He is grading our papers right now.   grading
9. She is weeving a placemat of ribbons.   weaving
10. What is the big deel anyway?   deal

31

Review

Directions: Circle the letters that spell the two ē vowels and three ā vowels in the sentence below.

Kay needs ice cream to go with her plain cake.

Directions: For the two bold words, write **N** over the noun and **V** over the verb. Combine the sentence pairs. Change each verb to include a helping verb such as **was** or **were** and add **ing**.

Example:
                V   N
My dad **taped** a TV **show**. It was a football game.

My dad was taping a TV show, a football game.

1. John **paddled** down the **stream**. John was our guide.
   John, our guide, was paddling down the stream.
2. He **weaved** a **present**. It was a present for his grandmother.
   He was weaving a placemat, a present for his grandmother.
3. Pete **claimed** he won the **game**. Pete is my neighbor.
   Pete, my neighbor, was claiming he had won the game.
4. My sister **treated** us to ice cream. My sister's name is **Polly**.
   Polly, my sister, was treating us to ice cream.
5. Maria **sneezed** while we were at the **fair**. Maria is my cousin.
   My cousin Maria was sneezing at the fair.
6. Julie and Kim **pounded** the **clay**. They are my twin sisters.
   Julie and Kim, my twin sisters, were pounding the clay.
7. Bobby **complained** about a **pain** in his foot. Bobby is the pitcher on our team.
   Bobby, our pitcher, was complaining about a pain in his foot.

32

Spelling: Long i and o

Long ī can be spelled **i** as in **wild**, **igh** as in **night**, **i-e** as in **wipe** or **y** as in **try**. Long ō can be spelled **o** as in **most**, **oa** as in **toast**, **ow** as in **throw** or **o-e** as in **hope**.

stripe	groan	glow	toast	grind	fry	sight	stove	toads	flight

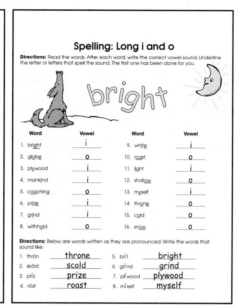

Directions: Complete the exercises with words from the box.

1. Write each word from the box with its vowel sound.

ī   stripe, grind, fry, sight, flight
ō   groan, glow, toast, stove, toads

2. Complete these sentences, using a word with the given vowel sound. Use each word from the box only once.

We will (ī) __fry__ potatoes on the (ō) __stove__

I thought I heard a low (ō) __groan__ , but when I looked, there was nothing

in (ī) __sight__ .

The airplane for our (ī) __flight__ had a (ī) __stripe__ painted on its side.

I saw a strange (ō) __glow__ coming from the toaster while

making (ō) __toast__

Do (ō) __toads__ live in the water like frogs?

We need to (ī) __grind__ up the nuts before we put them in the cookie dough.

33

Spelling: Long i and o

Directions: Read the words. After each word, write the correct vowel sound. Underline the letter or letters that spell the sound. The first one has been done for you.

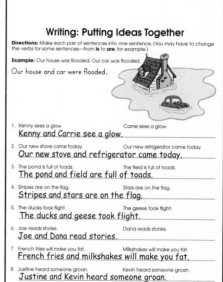
bright

	Word	Vowel		Word	Vowel
1.	br**igh**t	i	9.	wh**i**te	i
2.	gl**o**be	o	10.	r**oa**st	o
3.	pl**y**wood	i	11.	l**igh**t	i
4.	mank**i**nd	i	12.	shall**ow**	o
5.	c**oa**ching	o	13.	m**y**self	i
6.	pr**i**ze	i	14.	thr**o**ne	o
7.	gr**i**nd	i	15.	c**o**ld	o
8.	withh**o**ld	o	16.	sn**ow**	o

Directions: Below are words written as they are pronounced. Write the words that sound like:

1.	thrōn	throne	5.	brīt	bright
2.	skōld	scold	6.	grīnd	grind
3.	prīz	prize	7.	plī wood	plywood
4.	rōst	roast	8.	mī self	myself

34

Writing: Putting Ideas Together

Directions: Make each pair of sentences into one sentence. (You may have to change the verbs for some sentences—from **is** to **are**, for example.)

Example: Our house was flooded. Our car was flooded.
Our house and car were flooded.

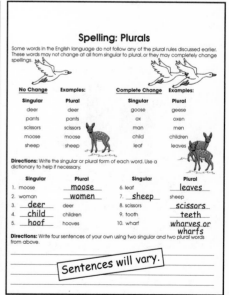

1. Kenny sees a glow.   Carrie sees a glow.
Kenny and Carrie see a glow.

2. Our new stove came today.   Our new refrigerator came today.
Our new stove and refrigerator came today.

3. The pond is full of toads.   The field is full of toads.
The pond and field are full of toads.

4. Stripes are on the flag.   Stars are on the flag.
Stripes and stars are on the flag.

5. The ducks took flight.   The geese took flight.
The ducks and geese took flight.

6. Joe reads stories.   Dana reads stories.
Joe and Dana read stories.

7. French fries will make you fat. Milkshakes will make you fat.
French fries and milkshakes will make you fat.

8. Justine heard someone groan.   Kevin heard someone groan.
Justine and Kevin heard someone groan.

35

Spelling: Plurals

Nouns come in two forms: singular and plural. When a noun is **singular**, it means there is only one person, place or thing.

Examples: car, swing, box, truck, slide, bus

When a noun is **plural**, it means there is more than one person, place or thing.

Examples: two cars, four trucks, three swings, five slides, six boxes, three buses

Usually an **s** is added to most nouns to make them plural. However, if the noun ends in **s**, **x**, **ch** or **sh**, then **es** is added to make it plural.

Directions: Write the singular or plural form of each word.

	Singular	Plural		Singular	Plural
1.	car	cars	9.	trick	tricks
2.	bush	bushes	10.	mess	messes
3.	wish	wishes	11.	box	boxes
4.	fox	foxes	12.	dish	dishes
5.	rule	rules	13.	boat	boats
6.	stitch	stitches	14.	path	paths
7.	switch	switches	15.	arm	arms
8.	barn	barns	16.	stick	sticks

Directions: Rewrite the following sentences and change the bold nouns from singular to plural or from plural to singular. The first one has been done for you.

1. She took a **book** to school.
She took books to school.

2. Tommy made **wishes** at his birthday party.
Tommy made a wish at his birthday party.

3. The **fox** ran away from the hunters.
The foxes ran away from the hunters.

4. The **houses** were painted white.
The house was painted white.

36

Spelling: Plurals

When a word ends with a consonant before **y**, to make it plural, drop the **y** and add **ies**.

Examples:
party → parties
cherry → cherries
daisy → daisies

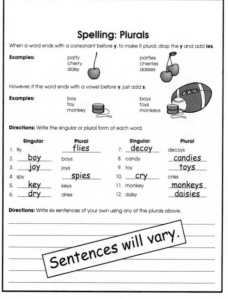

However, if the word ends with a vowel before **y**, just add **s**.

Examples:
boy → boys
toy → toys
monkey → monkeys

Directions: Write the singular or plural form of each word.

	Singular	Plural		Singular	Plural
1.	fly	flies	7.	decoy	decoys
2.	boy	boys	8.	candy	candies
3.	joy	joys	9.	toy	toys
4.	spy	spies	10.	cry	cries
5.	key	keys	11.	monkey	monkeys
6.	dry	dries	12.	daisy	daisies

Directions: Write six sentences of your own using any of the plurals above.

Sentences will vary.

37

Spelling: Plurals

Some words in the English language do not follow any of the plural rules discussed earlier. These words may not change at all from singular to plural, or they may completely change spellings.

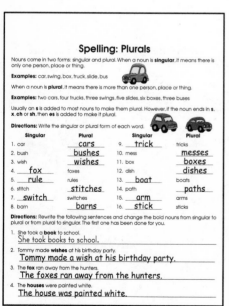

No Change		Examples:		Complete Change		Examples:
Singular		**Plural**		**Singular**		**Plural**
deer		deer		goose		geese
pants		pants		ox		oxen
scissors		scissors		man		men
moose		moose		child		children
sheep		sheep		leaf		leaves

Directions: Write the singular or plural form of each word. Use a dictionary to help if necessary.

	Singular	Plural		Singular	Plural
1.	moose	moose	6.	leaf	leaves
2.	woman	women	7.	sheep	sheep
3.	deer	deer	8.	scissors	scissors
4.	child	children	9.	tooth	teeth
5.	hoof	hooves	10.	wharf	wharves or wharfs

Directions: Write four sentences of your own using two singular and two plural words from above.

Sentences will vary.

38

Review

Review these rules for making singular words plural.

For most words, simply add **s.**
Examples: one book — two books   one house — four houses

For words ending with **s, ss, sh, ch** and **x,** add **es.**
Examples: one class — two classes   one church — three churches
one box — four boxes   one crash — five crashes

For words ending with a consonant before **y,** drop the **y** and add **ies.**
Examples: one daisy — three daisies   one cherry — two cherries

For words ending with a vowel before **y,** just add **s.**
Examples: one key — eight keys   one monkey — four monkeys

Directions: Write the singular or plural form of each word.

	Singular	Plural		Singular	Plural
1.	mattress	mattresses	10.	candy	candies
2.	bush	bushes	11.	try	tries
3.	sandwich	sandwiches	12.	turkey	turkeys
4.	fry	fries	13.	copy	copies
5.	cross	crosses	14.	factory	factories
6.	marsh	marshes	15.	fox	foxes
7.	supply	supplies	16.	ax	axes
8.	donkey	donkeys	17.	berry	berries
9.	stove	stoves	18.	day	days

39

Writing: Adjectives

Adjectives tell more about nouns. Adjectives are describing words.

Examples: scary animals   **bright** glow   **wet** frog

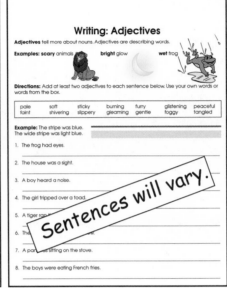

Directions: Add at least two adjectives to each sentence below. Use your own words or words from the box.

pale	soft	sticky	burning	furry	glistening	peaceful
faint	shivering	slippery	gleaming	gentle	foggy	tangled

Example: The stripe was blue.
The wide stripe was light blue.

1. The frog had eyes.

2. The house was a sight.

3. A boy heard a noise.

4. The girl tripped over a toad.

5. A tiger ran _Sentences will vary._

6. The _____

7. A par___ as sitting on the stove.

8. The boys were eating French fries.

40

Writing: Adjectives

Adjectives tell a noun's size, color, shape, texture, brightness, darkness, personality, sound, taste, and so on.

Examples: color — red, yellow, green, black
size — small, large, huge, tiny
shape — round, square, rectangular, oval
texture — rough, smooth, soft, scaly
brightness — glistening, shimmering, dull, pale
personality — gentle, grumpy, happy, sad

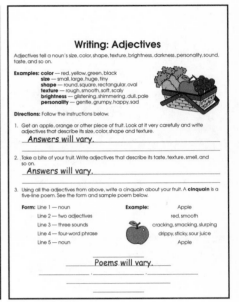

Directions: Follow the instructions below.

1. Get an apple, orange or other piece of fruit. Look at it very carefully and write adjectives that describe its size, color, shape and texture.
   Answers will vary.

2. Take a bite of your fruit. Write adjectives that describe its taste, texture, smell, and so on.
   Answers will vary.

3. Using all the adjectives from above, write a cinquain about your fruit. A **cinquain** is a five-line poem. See the form and sample poem below.

Form: Line 1 — noun	**Example:** Apple
Line 2 — two adjectives	red, smooth
Line 3 — three sounds	cracking, smacking, slurping
Line 4 — four-word phrase	drippy, sticky, sour juice
Line 5 — noun	Apple

Poems will vary.

41

Spelling: Long u

Long **ū** can be spelled, **u-e** as in **cube** or **ew** as in **few.** Some sounds are similar in sound to **u** but are not true **u** sounds, such as the **oo** in **tooth,** the **o-e** in **move** and the **ue** in **blue.**

Directions: Complete each sentence using a word from the box. Do not use the same word more than once.

| blew |
| tune |
| flute |
| cute |
| stew |
| June |
| glue |

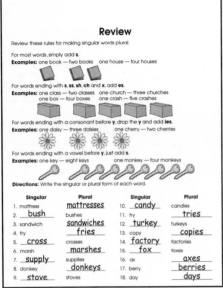

1. Yesterday, the wind **blew** so hard it knocked down a tree on our street.

2. My favorite instrument is the **flute** .

3. The little puppy in the window is so **cute** .

4. I love **June** because it's so warm, and we get out of school.

5. For that project, you will need scissors, construction paper and **glue** .

6. I recognize that song because it has a familiar **tune** .

7. My grandmother's beef **stew** is the best I've ever tasted.

42

Writing: Adverbs

Like adjectives, **adverbs** are describing words. They describe verbs. Adverbs tell how, when or where action takes place.

Examples: How	**When**	**Where**
slowly	yesterday	here
gracefully	today	there
swiftly	tomorrow	everywhere
quickly	soon	

How?
When?
Where?

Hint: To identify an adverb, locate the verb, then ask yourself if there are any words that tell how, when or where action takes place.

Directions: Read the following sentences. Underline the adverbs, then write whether they tell how, when or where. The first one has been done for you.

1. At the end of the day, the children ran <u>quickly</u> home from school.   how
2. They will have a spelling test <u>tomorrow</u>.   when
3. <u>Slowly</u>, the children filed to their seats.   how
4. The teacher sat <u>here</u> at her desk.   where
5. She will pass the tests back <u>later</u>.   when
6. The students received their grades <u>happily</u>.   how

Directions: Write four sentences of your own using any of the adverbs above.

Sentences will vary.

43

Writing: Using Adjectives and Adverbs

Directions: Complete these sentences by adding words that tell who, what, where or when.

Who or What		Where	When
tiger	stripe	out of sight	early in the morning
someone	groan	behind the door	when I wasn't looking
friend	glow	far away	late at night
sister	toad	very close	before I got there
brother	stove	up the stairs	when the moon was full

Example: They noticed a green glow behind the pine trees.
                                    (what)   (where)

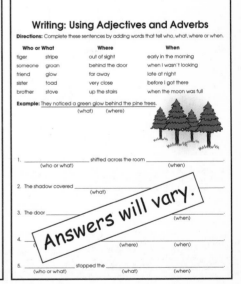

1. _____ shifted across the room _____
   (who or what)   (when)

2. The shadow covered _____
                            (what)

3. The door _____ _Answers will vary._
                                                   (when)

4. _____ _____ _____
        (where)   (when)

5. _____ stopped the _____ _____
   (who or what)   (what)   (when)

44

Page 45

Spelling: Vowel Sound Puzzle

Directions: Write the word from the box that answers each question.

| stripe | groan | toast | grind | fly | sight | stove | tune | flight |

Vowel Sounds

Vowel Sounds

Across:
Which word . . .
2. Begins like **toe** and rhymes with **most**?
4. Sounds the same as **grown**?
5. Begins like **stop** and rhymes with **cove**?
6. Begins like **flip** and rhymes with **kite**?

Down:
Which word . . .
1. Begins like **green** and rhymes with **find**?
2. Begins like **to** and rhymes with **moon**?
3. Begins like **stop** and rhymes with **type**?
5. Begins like **season** and rhymes with **bite**?
6. Begins like **feather** and rhymes with **pie**?

45

Page 46

Review

Directions: Circle the letters that spell three ō vowels, three ī vowels and one ū vowel in the sentence below.

Mōr hōpes his cōld tōad will be hōme bȳ tonīght.

Directions: Pretend something scary happened and you are asked to write about it for your school newspaper.

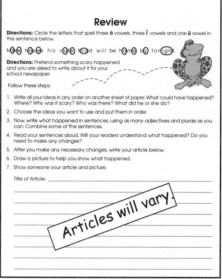

Follow these steps:

1. Write all your ideas in any order on another sheet of paper. What could have happened? Where? Why was it scary? Who was there? What did he or she do?
2. Choose the ideas you want to use and put them in order.
3. Now, write what happened in sentences, using as many adjectives and plurals as you can. Combine some of the sentences.
4. Read your sentences aloud. Will your readers understand what happened? Do you need to make any changes?
5. After you make any necessary changes, write your article below.
6. Draw a picture to help you show what happened.
7. Show someone your article and picture.

Title of Article: _____

Articles will vary.

46

Page 47

Spelling: The k Sound

The **k** sound can be spelled with **k** as in **peek**, **c** as in **cousin**, **ck** as in **sick**, **ch** as in **Chris** and **cc** as in **accuse**. In some words, however, one **c** may be pronounced **k** and the other **s** as in **accident**.

Directions: Answer the questions with words from the box.

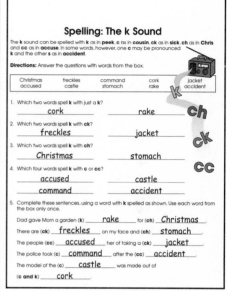

| Christmas | freckles | command | cork | jacket |
| accused | castle | stomach | rake | accident |

1. Which two words spell **k** with just a **k**?
   cork   rake

2. Which two words spell **k** with **ck**?
   freckles   jacket

3. Which two words spell **k** with **ch**?
   Christmas   stomach

4. Which four words spell **k** with **c** or **cc**?
   accused   castle
   command   accident

5. Complete these sentences, using a word with **k** spelled as shown. Use each word from the box only once.

Dad gave Mom a garden (k) rake for (ch) Christmas

There are (ck) freckles on my face and (ch) stomach

The people (cc) accused her of taking a (ck) jacket

The police took (c) command after the (cc) accident

The model of the (c) castle was made out of

(c and k) cork .

47

Page 48

Spelling: The k Sound

Directions: Underline the letters that spell **k** in each word. The first one has been done for you.

1. toothpi**ck**
2. ar**c**
3. **k**itchen
4. a**cc**laim
5. a**cc**ount
6. **Ch**ristmas
7. ma**k**e
8. **c**onfirm
9. bri**ck**
10. stoma**ch**

toothpick
c – k

Directions: Under each spelling for **k**, write five words that have the same **k** spellings.

k	ck	c	ch	cc
	sickness			
Answers will vary.				mical
kite				accumulate

Directions: See how many words you can write that have the **cc** spelling, with one **c** pronounced **k** and the other pronounced **s**.

Answers may include: accept, accent, access, accompany

48

Page 49

Writing: Using Conjunctions

Conjunctions are joining words that can be used to combine sentences. Words such as **and**, **but**, **or**, **when** and **after** are conjunctions.

Examples:
Sally went to the mall. She went to the movies.
Sally went to the mall, and she went to the movies.

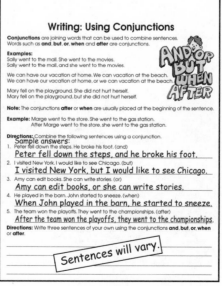
AND OR BUT WHEN AFTER

We can have our vacation at home. We can vacation at the beach.
We can have our vacation at home, or we can vacation at the beach.

Mary fell on the playground. She did not hurt herself.
Mary fell on the playground, but she did not hurt herself.

Note: The conjunctions **after** or **when** are usually placed at the beginning of the sentence.

Example: Marge went to the store. She went to the gas station.
After Marge went to the store, she went to the gas station.

Directions: Combine the following sentences using a conjunction.
Sample answers:
1. Peter fell down the steps. He broke his foot. (and)
   Peter fell down the steps, and he broke his foot.
2. I visited New York. I would like to see Chicago. (but)
   I visited New York, but I would like to see Chicago.
3. Amy can edit books. She can write stories. (or)
   Amy can edit books, or she can write stories.
4. He played in the barn. John started to sneeze. (when)
   When John played in the barn, he started to sneeze.
5. The team won the playoffs. They went to the championships. (after)
   After the team won the playoffs, they went to the championships.

Directions: Write three sentences of your own using the conjunctions **and**, **but**, **or**, **when** or **after**.

Sentences will vary.

49

Page 50

Writing: Using Conjunctions

Directions: Combine each pair of sentences using the conjunctions **or**, **and**, **but**, **after** or **when**. You may need to change the word order in the sentences.

Examples:
My stomach hurts.   I still want to go to the movies.
My stomach hurts, but I still want to go to the movies.

Sample answers:
1. He accused me of peeking.   I felt very angry.
   When he accused me of peeking, I felt very angry.
2. The accident was over.   I started shaking.
   After the accident was over, I started shaking.
3. Is that a freckle?   Is that dirt?
   Is that a freckle or is that dirt?
4. I forgot my jacket.   I had to go back and get it.
   I forgot my jacket, and I had to go back and get it.
5. I like Christmas.   I don't like waiting for it.
   I like Christmas, but I don't like waiting for it.
6. Would you like to live in a castle?   Would you like to live on a houseboat?
   Would you like to live in a castle, or would you like to live on a houseboat?
7. The general gave the command.   The army marched.
   When the general gave the command, the army marched.
8. The trees dropped all their leaves.   We raked them up.
   After the trees dropped all their leaves, we raked them up.

50

Page 51

Writing: Using ing Verbs

Remember, use **is** and **are** when describing something happening right now. Use **was** and **were** when describing something that already happened.

Directions: Use the verb on the left to complete each sentence. Add **ing** to the verb and use **is, are, was** or **were**.

Examples:
When it started to rain, we **were raking** the leaves.
rake

When the soldiers marched up that hill, Captain Stevens **was commanding** them.
command

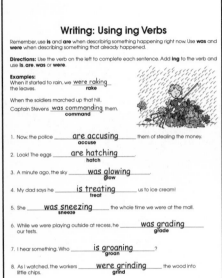

1. Now, the police **are accusing** them of stealing the money.
accuse

2. Look! The eggs **are hatching**
hatch

3. A minute ago, the sky **was glowing**
glow

4. My dad says he **is treating** us to ice cream!
treat

5. She **was sneezing** the whole time we were at the mall.
sneeze

6. While we were playing outside at recess, he **was grading** our tests.
grade

7. I hear something. Who **is groaning** ?
groan

8. As I watched, the workers **were grinding** the wood into little chips.
grind

51

Page 52

Writing: Using ing Verbs

Using **ing** verbs can make your writing more interesting to read. Compare these lists of verbs:

List A	List B
went	skipping
look	discovering
find	digging
sleep	snoring
run	slithering
drop	sailing
go	soaring

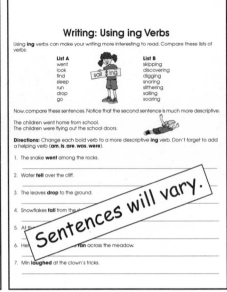

Now, compare these sentences. Notice that the second sentence is much more descriptive.

The children went home from school.
The children were flying out the school doors.

Directions: Change each bold verb to a more descriptive **ing** verb. Don't forget to add a helping verb (**am, is, are, was, were**).

1. The snake **went** among the rocks.

2. Water **fell** over the cliff.

3. The leaves **drop** to the ground.

4. Snowflakes **fall** from the

5. At the

6. Her **ran** across the meadow.

7. Min **laughed** at the clown's tricks.

Sentences will vary.

52

Page 53

Writing: Using ing Verbs

Directions: Using descriptive **ing** verbs, write five sentences about activities you do every day.

Example: Peter ate his breakfast.
Peter is scarfing down his breakfast so he won't miss the bus.

Sentences will vary.

Directions: Use **ing** verbs to write a cinquain. Then draw a picture to go with it.

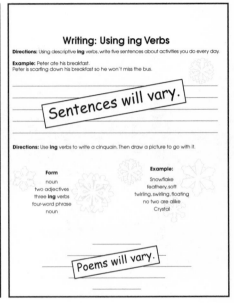

Form	Example:
noun	Snowflake
two adjectives	feathery, soft
three **ing** verbs	twirling, swirling, floating
four-word phrase	no two are alike
noun	Crystal

Poems will vary.

53

Page 54

Writing: Using Conjunctions

Directions: Combine each pair of sentences, choosing the best joining words. Here are some choices: **and, but, or, when** and **after**. You may need to change the sentence order.

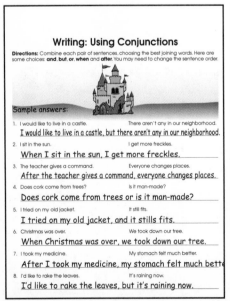

Sample answers:

1. I would like to live in a castle.   There aren't any in our neighborhood.
   I would like to live in a castle, but there aren't any in our neighborhood.

2. I sit in the sun.   I get more freckles.
   When I sit in the sun, I get more freckles.

3. The teacher gives a command.   Everyone changes places.
   After the teacher gives a command, everyone changes places.

4. Does cork come from trees?   Is it man-made?
   Does cork come from trees or is it man-made?

5. I tried on my old jacket.   It still fits.
   I tried on my old jacket, and it stills fits.

6. Christmas was over.   We took down our tree.
   When Christmas was over, we took down our tree.

7. I took my medicine.   My stomach felt much better.
   After I took my medicine, my stomach felt much bette

8. I'd like to rake the leaves.   It's raining now.
   I'd like to rake the leaves, but it's raining now.

54

Page 55

Spelling: Finding Mistakes

Directions: Circle the spelling mistakes. Then write the words correctly.

1. What did you get for Cristmas this year?   Christmas
2. My aunt gave me boots and a new jaket.   jacket
3. I need to get some food in my stomack.   stomach
4. Does anyone know why korks float?   corks
5. I dropped my glass by accident.   accident
6. A comand is a sentence that tells someone to do something.   command
7. We visited a casel on our trip to Ireland.   castle
8. My big brother is always acusing me of using his stuff.   accusing
9. I lost the rak under all the leaves.   rake
10. I wish I had as many frekles as you.   freckles

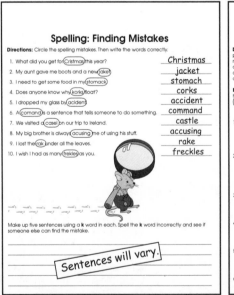

Make up five sentences using a **k** word in each. Spell the **k** word incorrectly and see if someone else can find the mistake.

Sentences will vary.

55

Page 56

Writing: Punctuation

Directions: In the paragraphs below, use periods, question marks or exclamation marks to show where one sentence ends and the next begins. Circle the first letter of each new sentence to show the capital.

Example: My sister accused me of not helping her rake the leaves, that's silly! I helped at least a hundred times.

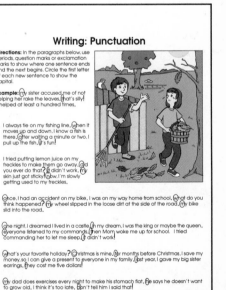

1. I always tie on my fishing line, when it moves up and down, I know a fish is there. After waiting a minute or two, I pull up the fish. It's fun!

2. I tried putting lemon juice on my freckles to make them go away. Did you ever do that? It didn't work. My skin just got sticky. Now, I'm slowly getting used to my freckles.

3. Once, I had an accident on my bike. I was on my way home from school. What do you think happened? My wheel slipped in the loose dirt at the side of the road. My bike slid into the road.

4. One night, I dreamed I lived in a castle. In my dream, I was the king or maybe the queen. Everyone listened to my commands. Then Mom woke me up for school. I tried commanding her to let me sleep. It didn't work!

5. What's your favorite holiday? Christmas is mine. For months before Christmas, I save my money, so I can give a present to everyone in my family. Last year, I gave my big sister earrings. They cost me five dollars!

6. My dad does exercises every night to make his stomach flat. He says he doesn't want to grow old. I think it's too late. Don't tell him I said that!

56

Writing: Punctuation

Directions: In the paragraphs below, use periods, question marks and exclamation marks to show where one sentence ends and the next begins. Circle the first letter of each new sentence to show the capital.

1. It was Christmas Eve. Santa and the elves were loading the toys onto his sleigh. The deer keepers were harnessing the reindeer and walking them toward the sleigh.

2. The reindeer were prancing with anxious anticipation of their midnight flight. Soon, the sleigh was overflowing with its load, and Santa was ready to travel. Crack went his whip! The reindeer pulled and tugged against their harnesses. The sleigh inched forward, slowly at first, then swiftly it climbed into the holiday night sky.

3. Everything was going smoothly. Santa and the reindeer made excellent time traveling from house to house and city to city. At each home, of course, the children had left Santa snacks of cookies and milk.

4. Around 2 o'clock in the morning, Santa felt his red suit begin to get tight around his middle. "Hmmm," he said to himself, "I have been eating too many snacks." He decided that after the next house he would have to cut back on his cookie calories.

5. The reindeer team guided Santa to his next stop. He hopped out of his sleigh, grabbed his bundle of toys and jogged to the chimney. He climbed up to the chimney's opening and started down to the fireplace. Oops! Something awful happened. Santa got stuck! Oh, no! What do we do now, wondered the reindeer?

Directions: Complete the story about Santa. Use your knowledge of adjectives, adverbs and descriptive verbs to make your story more interesting and fun to read.

57

Spelling: Figuring Out the Code

Remember that the vowels are **a, e, i, o, u** and sometimes **y**. All the other letters are consonants.

Directions: Each picture below stands for a consonant. Write the consonant it stands for on the line. Then add vowels to spell words from the box.

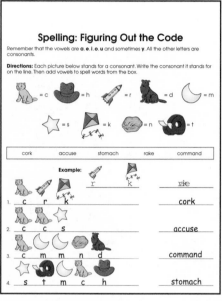

| cork | accuse | stomach | rake | command |

Example:

	r	k	ra̲k̲e̲	

1. c r k _____ cork
2. c c s _____ accuse
3. c m m n d _____ command
4. s t m c h _____ stomach

58

Writing: Story Map

A **story map** helps to organize your thoughts in a logical sequence before you begin to write a story or report.

Directions: Use the following story map to arrange your thoughts for the police report on page 60.

Characters: Setting: (time, place)

Problem: (what needs to be fixed or solved)

Goal:

Action: (events, reasons)

Outcome: (results of action)

Story maps will vary.

59

Review

Directions: Write a police report about an event in which someone your age was a hero or heroine. Follow these steps:

1. Write all your ideas in any order on another sheet of paper. What happened? Who saw it? Who or what do you think caused it? Why were the police called?

2. Choose the ideas you want to use and organize them with the story map on page 59.

3. Now, write in complete sentences to tell what happened. Combine some short sentences using **and, but, or, after** or **when**. Make sure all your sentences end with a period or question mark.

4. Read your sentences aloud. Did you leave out any important facts? Will your "commanding officer" know what happened?

5. Make any necessary changes and write your report below.

6. Read your report to someone.

OFFICIAL POLICE REPORT

Reporting officer: _____

Date of accident: _____   Time of accident: _____

Reports will vary.

60

Spelling: The f Sound

The **f** sound can be spelled with **f** as in **fun, gh** as in **laugh** or **ph** as in **phone**.

Directions: Answer the questions with words from the box.

| fuss | paragraph | phone | friendship | freedom |
| defend | flood | alphabet | rough | laughter |

1. Which three words spell **f** with **ph**?

____paragraph____ ____phone____ ____alphabet____

2. Which two words spell **f** with **gh**?

____rough____ ____laughter____

3. Which five words spell **f** with an **f**?

____fuss____ ____defend____ ____flood____
____friendship____ ____freedom____

4. Complete these sentences, using a word with **f** spelled as shown. Use each word from the box only once.

I don't know why my teacher makes so much (**f**) ____fuss____ over writing
a (**ph**) ____paragraph____ .

A (**f**) ____friendship____ can help you through (**gh**) ____rough____ times.

The soldiers will (**f**) ____defend____ our (**f**) ____freedom____ .

Can you say the (**ph**) ____alphabet____ backwards?

When I answered the (**ph**) ____phone____ , all I could
hear was (**gh**) ____laughter____ .

If it keeps raining, we'll have a (**f**) ____flood____ .

61

Spelling: The f Sound

Directions: Read the following words. Underline the letters that spell **f** in each word.

1. laughter
2. football
3. cough
4. paragraph
5. enough
6. phantom
7. roof
8. performance
9. toughest
10. telephone
11. before
12. roughness
13. alphabet
14. grief
15. graph

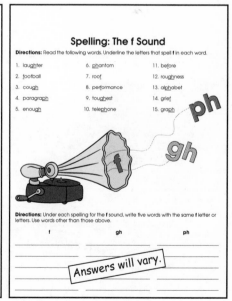

Directions: Under each spelling for the **f** sound, write five words with the same **f** letter or letters. Use words other than those above.

f   gh   ph

Answers will vary.

62

Writing: Topic Sentences

A **paragraph** is a group of sentences that tells about one main idea. A **topic sentence** tells the main idea of a paragraph.

Many topic sentences come first in the paragraph. The topic sentence in the paragraph below is underlined. Do you see how it tells the reader what the whole paragraph is about?

<u>Friendships can make you happy or make you sad.</u> You feel happy to do things and go places with your friends. You get to know each other so well that you can almost read each others' minds. But friendships can be sad when your friend moves away—or decides to be best friends with someone else.

Directions: Underline the topic sentence in the paragraph below.

<u>We have two rules about using the phone at our house.</u> Our whole family agreed on them. The first rule is not to talk longer than 10 minutes. The second rule is to take good messages if you answer the phone for someone else.

Directions: After you read the paragraph below, write a topic sentence for it.

There are many ways you can earn money.

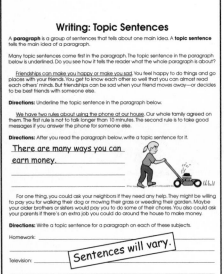

For one thing, you could ask your neighbors if they need any help. They may be willing to pay you for walking their dog or mowing their grass or weeding their garden. Maybe your older brothers or sisters would pay you to do some of their chores. You also could ask your parents if there's an extra job you could do around the house to make money.

Directions: Write a topic sentence for a paragraph on each of these subjects.

Homework: _____

Television: _____

Sentences will vary.

63

Writing: Supporting Sentences

Supporting sentences provide details about the topic sentence of a paragraph.

Directions: In the paragraph below, underline the topic sentence. Then cross out the supporting sentence that does not belong in the paragraph.

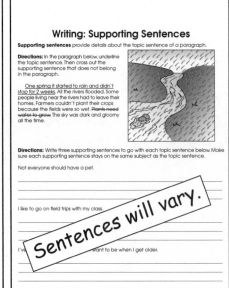

<u>One spring it started to rain and didn't stop for 2 weeks.</u> All the rivers flooded. Some people living near the rivers had to leave their homes. Farmers couldn't plant their crops because the fields were so wet. ~~Plants need water to grow.~~ The sky was dark and gloomy all the time.

Directions: Write three supporting sentences to go with each topic sentence below. Make sure each supporting sentence stays on the same subject as the topic sentence.

Not everyone should have a pet.

_____

I like to go on field trips with my class.

_____

I've _____ want to be when I get older.

Sentences will vary.

64

Writing: Topic Sentences and Supporting Details

Directions: For each topic below, write a topic sentence and four supporting details.

Example:
Playing with friends: (topic sentence) Playing with my friends can be lots of fun.
(details)
1. We like to ride our bikes together.
2. We play fun games like "dress up" and "animal hospital."
3. Sometimes, we swing on the swings or slide down the slides on our swingsets.
4. We like to pretend we are having tea with our stuffed animals.

Recess at school: _____

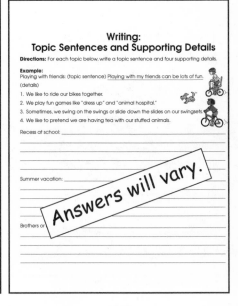

Summer vacation: _____

Brothers or _____

Answers will vary.

65

Writing:
Topic Sentences and Supporting Details

Directions: Select a topic from page 65. Arrange the topic sentence and detail sentences in paragraph form.

Example: Playing With Friends
Playing with my friends can be lots of fun. We play fun games like animal hospital and "dress up." We like to pretend we are having tea with our stuffed animals. Sometimes, we swing on the swings or slide down the slides on our swingsets. We also like to ride our bikes together.

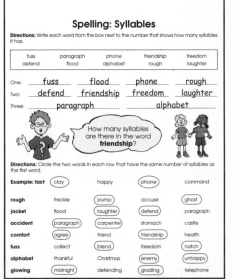

Note: Notice how the first line of the paragraph is indented. Also note how the order of the sentences changed to make the paragraph easier to read.

Directions: Choose a topic. Write a five-sentence paragraph about it. Don't forget the topic sentence, supporting details and to indent your paragraph. Make sure the detail sentences stick to the topic.

_____

Paragraphs will vary.

66

Spelling: Syllables

A **syllable** is a word—or part of a word—with only one vowel sound. Some words have just one syllable, such as **cat**, **dog** and **house**. Some words have two syllables, such as **in-sist** and **be-fore**. Some words have three syllables, such as **re-mem-ber**; four syllables, such as **un-der-stand-ing**; or more. Often words are easier to spell if you know how many syllables they have.

Syl-la-bles

Directions: Write the number of syllables in each word below.

Word	Syllables		Word	Syllables
1. amphibian	4	11.	want	1
2. liter	2	12.	communication	5
3. guild	1	13.	pedestrian	4
4. chili	2	14.	kilo	2
5. vegetarian	5	15.	autumn	2
6. comedian	4	16.	dinosaur	3
7. warm	1	17.	grammar	2
8. piano	3	18.	dry	1
9. barbarian	4	19.	solar	2
10. chef	1	20.	wild	1

Directions: Next to each number, write words with the same number of syllables.

1. _____
2. _____
3. _____
4. _____
5. _____

Answers will vary.

67

Spelling: Syllables

Directions: Write each word from the box next to the number that shows how many syllables it has.

fuss	paragraph	phone	friendship	freedom
defend	flood	alphabet	rough	laughter

One: fuss   flood   phone   rough
Two: defend   friendship   freedom   laughter
Three: paragraph   alphabet

How many syllables are there in the word **friendship**?

Directions: Circle the two words in each row that have the same number of syllables as the first word.

Example: fact	(clay)	happy	(phone)	command
rough	freckle	(pump)	accuse	(ghost)
jacket	flood	(laughter)	(defend)	paragraph
accident	(paragraph)	(carpenter)	stomach	castle
comfort	(agree)	friend	(friendship)	health
fuss	collect	(blend)	freedom	hatch
alphabet	thankful	Christmas	(enemy)	unhappy
glowing	(midnight)	defending	(grading)	telephone

68

Spelling: Searching for Words

Directions: Make a word search using words from the box. First, print the words in the spaces below, making some of them cross each other. Then fill the extra spaces with other letters.

Example:

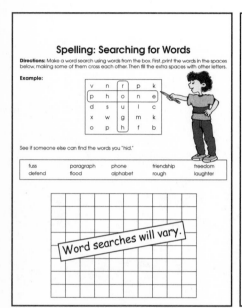

v	n	r	p	k
p	h	o	n	e
d	s	u	l	c
x	w	g	m	k
o	p	h	f	b

See if someone else can find the words you "hid."

fuss	paragraph	phone	friendship	freedom
defend	flood	alphabet	rough	laughter

Word searches will vary.

69

Writing: Paragraphs

Each paragraph should have one main idea. If you have a lot of ideas, you need to write several paragraphs.

Directions: Read the ideas below and number them:
1. If the idea tells about Jill herself.
2. If the idea tells what she did.
3. If the idea tells why she did it.

2 _ found a bird caught in a kite string

2 or 1 _ plays outside a lot

1 _ in grade four at Center School

3 _ knew the bird was wild

2 _ untangled the bird

1 _ likes pets

3 _ wouldn't want to live in a cage

2 _ gave the bird its freedom

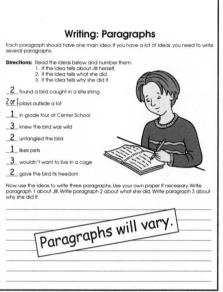

Now, use the ideas to write three paragraphs. Use your own paper if necessary. Write paragraph 1 about Jill. Write paragraph 2 about what she did. Write paragraph 3 about why she did it.

Paragraphs will vary.

70

Writing: Paragraphs

When you have many good ideas about a subject, you need to organize your writing into more than one paragraph. It is easy to organize your thoughts about a topic if you use a "cluster of ideas" chart.

Example:

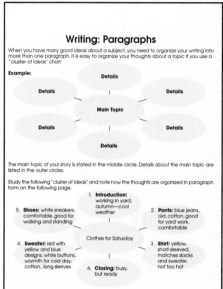

The main topic of your story is stated in the middle circle. Details about the main topic are listed in the outer circles.

Study the following "cluster of ideas" and note how the thoughts are organized in paragraph form on the following page.

1. **Introduction:** working in yard, autumn—cool weather

2. **Pants:** blue jeans, old, cotton, good for yard work, comfortable

3. **Shirt:** yellow, short-sleeved, matches slacks and sweater, not too hot

Clothes for Saturday

4. **Sweater:** red with yellow and blue designs, white buttons, warmth for cold day, cotton, long sleeves

5. **Shoes:** white sneakers, comfortable, good for walking and standing

6. **Closing:** busy, but ready

71

Writing: Paragraphs

Once your ideas are "clustered," go back and decide which ideas should be the first, second, third, and so on. These numbers will be the order of the paragraph in the finished story.

Directions: Read the story paragraphs below.

Clothes for Saturday

This Saturday, my family and I will be working in the yard. We will be mowing grass, raking leaves and pulling weeds. When I get up that day, I know I will need to wear clothes that will keep me warm in the autumn air. My clothes will also need to be ones that will not be ruined if they get muddy or dirty.

The best choice of pants for our busy day will be my jeans. They are nicely faded and well worn, which means they are quite comfortable. They will be good for yard work since mud and grass stains wash out of them easily.

My shirt will be my yellow golf shirt. It will match the blue of my jeans. Also, its short sleeves will be fine if the weather is warm.

For warmth on Saturday, if the day is cool, will be my yellow and red sweater. It is made from cotton and has long sleeves and high buttons to keep out frosty air.

Yard work means lots of walking, so I will need comfortable shoes. The best choice will be my white sneakers. They aren't too tight or too loose and keep my feet strong.

Saturday will be a busy day, but I'll be ready!

When "Clothes for Saturday" was written, the author added both an introductory and concluding paragraph. This helps the reader with the flow of the story.

Directions: Now, it's your turn. Select a topic from the list below or choose one of your own. Complete the "cluster of ideas" chart on page 73 and write a brief story. (You may or may not use all the clusters.)

Topics:

chores	holidays	all about me	sports
homework	family	pets	vacation

72

Writing: Cluster of Ideas

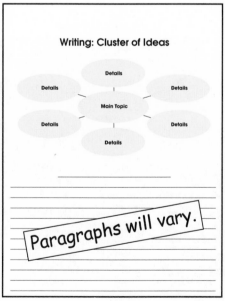

Paragraphs will vary.

73

Spelling: Unscrambling Letters

Directions: Put the letters in order to spell the **f** words. If you need help with spelling, look on page 61.

feeddn	defend	odolf	flood
nopeh	phone	dspiienthr	friendship
gletharu	laughter	gruho	rough
ssfu	fuss	taalbehp	alphabet
droefem	freedom	ghaaprpar	paragraph

RT UAH P GBLRT

Directions: Use the correctly spelled word to answer the questions.

1. Which two words each have one syllable and spell **f** with an **f**?
   fuss, flood

2. Which word has two syllables and spells **f** with **gh**? _laughter_

3. Which word has one syllable and spells **f** with **ph**? _phone_

4. Which three words each have two syllables and spell **f** with an **f**?
   defend, freedom, friendship

5. Which two words each have three syllables and spell **f** with a **ph**?
   alphabet, paragraph

6. Which word has one syllable and spells **f** with **gh**? _rough_

74

Page 75 — Review

Directions: On another sheet of paper, write three paragraphs that tell a story about the picture below. Tell who lives in the house, what happened and why it happened. Begin each paragraph with a topic sentence that tells the main idea. Try to include some words with the **s** sound in them. Read your paragraphs aloud, make any necessary changes and copy them below.

Who lives there:

_____

What happened:

Paragraphs will vary.

Why it happened:

_____

75

Page 76 — Spelling: The s Sound

The **s** sound can be spelled with **s** as in **super** or **ss** as in **assign**. **c** as in **city**, **ce** as in **fence** or **sc** as in **scene**. In some words, though, **sc** is pronounced **sk**, as in **scare**.

Directions: Answer the questions using words from the box.

exciting	medicine	lettuce	peace	scissors
slice	scientist	sauce	bracelet	distance

1. Which five words spell **s** with just an **s** or **ss**?
   slice   sauce   distance
   scissors   scientist

2. Which two words spell **s** with just a **c**?
   exciting   medicine

3. Which six words spell **s** with a **ce**?
   slice   sauce   bracelet
   lettuce   peace   distance

4. Which two words spell **s** with **sc**?
   scientist   scissors

5. Complete these sentences, using a word with **s** spelled as shown. Use each word from the box only once.
   My (**ce**) __bracelet__ fell off my wrist into the tomato __sauce__ (**s and ce**).
   My salad was just a (**s and ce**) __slice__ of (**ce**) __lettuce__.
   It was (**c**) __exciting__ to see the lions, even though they were a long (**s and ce**) __distance__ away.
   The (**sc and s**) __scientist__ invented a new (**c**) __medicine__.
   If I lend you my (**sc and ss**) __scissors__, will you leave me in (**ce**) __peace__?

76

Page 77 — Spelling: The s Sound

Directions: Read the following words. Underline the letters that spell **s** in each word. In some words, more than one letter will be underlined.

1. impa<u>ss</u>ive
2. pla<u>c</u>ement
3. que<u>s</u>tion
4. con<u>sc</u>ious
5. ex<u>c</u>ellen<u>ce</u>
6. a<u>ss</u>ertive
7. <u>sc</u>epter
8. <u>sc</u>oundrel
9. a<u>ss</u>ortment
10. ignoran<u>ce</u>
11. pre<u>c</u>ious
12. judi<u>c</u>ious
13. differen<u>ce</u>
14. lifele<u>ss</u>
15. <u>s</u>olvent
16. <u>s</u>cope
17. ca<u>s</u>tle
18. <u>s</u>camper
19. <u>s</u>ociable
20. amu<u>s</u>ement
21. <u>s</u>cissors
22. in<u>s</u>uran<u>ce</u>
23. <u>s</u>camp
24. <u>s</u>cience

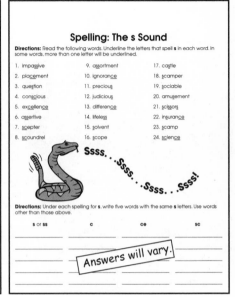

Directions: Under each spelling for **s**, write five words with the same **s** letters. Use words other than those above.

s or ss	c	ce	sc

Answers will vary.

77

Page 78 — Writing: Cause and Effect

Sometimes one sentence names an **effect** (something that happens) and another sentence tells what caused it. The **cause** is the reason something happens. Use the word **because** to combine them.

Example:
He was crying. (effect)
He fell off his bike. (cause)
He was crying because he fell off his bike.

Directions: Draw a line from each effect on the left to its cause on the right.

1. I didn't finish my project — because I like to experiment.
2. I have to take medicine — because today is her birthday.
3. I want to be a scientist — because I can't find scissors.
4. I gave my sister a bracelet — because my throat hurts.

The cause can also be written and combined with the word **so**.

Example:
Today is my sister's birthday, so I gave her a bracelet.
(cause)   (effect)

Sample answers:

Directions: Write the other three sentences from above with the cause first.

1. I like to experiment, so I want to be a scientist.

2. I can't find my scissors, so I didn't finish my project.

3. My throat hurts, so I have to take medicine.

78

Page 79 — Spelling: Listening for Sounds and Syllables

Directions: Answer the questions using words from the box.

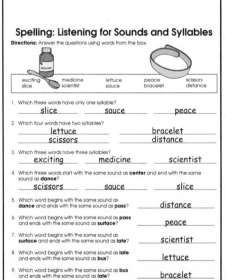

exciting	medicine	lettuce	peace	scissors
slice	scientist	sauce	bracelet	distance

1. Which three words have only one syllable?
   slice   sauce   peace

2. Which four words have two syllables?
   lettuce   bracelet
   scissors   distance

3. Which three words have three syllables?
   exciting   medicine   scientist

4. Which three words start with the same sound as **center** and end with the same sound as **dance**?
   scissors   sauce   slice

5. Which word begins with the same sound as **dance** and ends with the same sound as **pass**?
   distance

6. Which word begins with the same sound as **pass** and ends with the same sound as **surface**?
   peace

7. Which word begins with the same sound as **surface** and ends with the same sound as **late**?
   scientist

8. Which word begins with the same sound as **late** and ends with the same sound as **bus**?
   lettuce

9. Which word begins with the same sound as **bus** and ends with the same sound as **late**?
   bracelet

79

Page 80 — Writing: Writing Sentences Two Ways

Directions: Combine each pair of sentences in two ways. Write the cause first, then the effect first.

Example: Please buy more lettuce. Aunt Ethel likes salad.

   a. Aunt Ethel likes salad, so buy more lettuce.
      (cause)   (effect)

   b. Buy more lettuce because Aunt Ethel likes salad.
      (effect)   (cause)

1. We had to walk a long distance. The car broke down.
   a. The car broke down, so we had to walk a long distance.
   b. We had to walk a long distance because the car broke down.

2. I couldn't make snowballs. I forgot to bring my mittens.
   a. I forgot to bring my mittens, so I couldn't make snowballs.
   b. I couldn't make snowballs because I forgot my mittens.

3. I have to finish my report. I need peace and quiet.
   a. I have to finish my report, so I need peace and quiet.
   b. I need peace and quiet because I have to finish my report.

4. Cut the pie in eight slices. There are eight of us.
   a. There are eight of us, so cut the pie in eight slices.
   b. Cut the pie in eight slices because there are eight of us.

5. We are out of cheese sauce. I will make some more.
   a. We are out of cheese sauce, so I will make some more.
   b. I will make some more because we are out of cheese sauce.

80

Writing: Cause and Effect

Directions: Add a cause to each sentence.

Example: The nations were at peace **because the war was finally over.**

1. Mike's story was exciting _____

2. Anna couldn't cut her cake in slices _____

3. I asked Mom for some medicine _____

4. I don't like lettuce _____

Directions: _____ sentence.

Example: _____ was distracted, **so she made a mistake.**

1. I had run for a long distance _____

2. The sauce cooked too long _____

3. Ryan's scissors were dull _____

4. The bracelet was expensive _____

Answers will vary.

81

Spelling: Possessives

A **possessive noun** shows that something belongs to the noun. To show possession with singular nouns, an **apostrophe** and **s** are usually added.

Examples: Doug's coat   dog's leg

To show possession with a plural noun that ends with **s**, place an apostrophe after the **s**.

Examples: girls' papers   birds' food

To show possession with a plural noun that doesn't end with **s**, add an apostrophe and **s**.

Examples: men's shirts   mice's hole

Directions: Write the form of the word that is missing.

Singular	Singular Possessive	Plural	Plural Possessive
horse	horse's	horses	horses'
girl	girl's	girls	girls'
mouse	mouse's	mice	mice's
fish	fish's	fish	fish's
baby	baby's	babies	babies'
child	child's	children	children's
man	man's	men	men's

Directions: Complete the sentences with the correct form of the given word.

1. (Julie) What happened to _Julie's_ slice of cake?
2. (mother) Did you taste my _mother's_ sauce?
3. (child) The library has many exciting _children's_ books.

82

Spelling: Telling Plurals From Possessives

Remember: A noun is possessive when something belongs to it. A plural refers to more than one thing.

Examples: girls branches foxes

You also know we show possession by adding:
• an apostrophe and **s** to singular nouns: girl's child's
• just an apostrophe to plural nouns that end in **s**: girls'
• an apostrophe and **s** to plural nouns that don't end in **s**: children's women's

Directions: In each pair of sentences below, the given word should be plural in one and plural possessive in the other. Decide which is which and write the correct forms.

Example: (girls)   The girls decided to return to camp. The girls' tent had blown down.

1. (boys)   Please refill the _boys'_ glasses.
   Did the _boys_ say when they were coming?
2. (reporters)   _Reporters_ shouldn't misspell words.
   Where are the _reporters'_ notes?
3. (teachers)   Where will the _teachers_ eat?
   Did you misplace the _teachers'_ lunches?
4. (men)   Two _men_ were unable to lift it.
   The _men's_ ride was late.
5. (scientists)   The _scientists'_ report was full of facts.
   The _scientists_ had many opinions.
6. (children)   It's time to call the _children_.
   Did you read the _children's_ stories?

83

Spelling: S Sound Crossword Puzzle

Directions: Complete the puzzle below with **s** words.

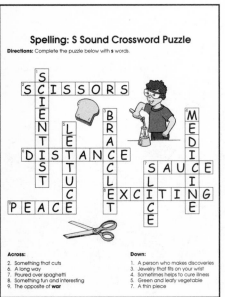

Across:
2. Something that cuts
6. A long way
7. Poured over spaghetti
8. Something fun and interesting
9. The opposite of **war**

Down:
1. A person who makes discoveries
3. Jewelry that fits on your wrist
4. Sometimes helps to cure illness
5. Green and leafy vegetable
7. A thin piece

84

Review

Directions: Follow these steps to complete the story:

1. Read the beginning of the story below and think about what might happen next. These ideas may help you get started:
   She was worried about what might happen, so . . .
   Later she found out it worked as medicine for . . .
   Her discovery was exciting because . . .
   People came great distances to . . .
2. Write ideas for your story on another sheet of paper.
3. Choose the ideas you want to use and group them into paragraphs, with one main idea in each paragraph.
4. Write the story in sentences. Remember to combine some of the sentences that explain cause and effect. Use a possessive noun at least twice.
5. Read your story aloud. Is it clear what happened? Are your ideas in order? Does your story have an ending?
6. Write your story below, using more paper if needed.
7. Let someone read your story.

One day, by accident, a scientist named Susan dropped some lettuce from her sandwich into a special experiment. As Susan watched. . . .

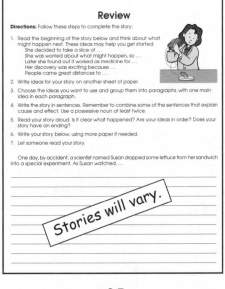

Stories will vary.

85

Spelling: Prefixes

A **prefix** is a syllable added to the beginning of a word that changes its meaning.
The prefix **un** means "not." **Unmade** means "not made."
The prefix **re** means "back" or "again." **Return** means "turn back."
The prefix **mis** means "wrong." **Mispronounce** means "pronounce wrong."

Directions: Add each prefix to the word to form a new word. Then write what the new word means.

Example	Words	Meaning
un + known =	unknown	not known
re + place =	replace	place back
mis + spell =	misspell	spell wrong
un + able =	unable	not able
re + pay =	repay	pay again
mis + use =	misuse	use wrong
un + usual =	unusual	not usual
re + view =	review	view again
mis + place =	misplace	place wrong
re + fill =	refill	fill again
un + sure =	unsure	not sure

Directions: Add **un, re** or **mis** to each given word.

1. It's (usual) _unusual_ when I (spell) _misspell_ a word.
2. We have to (place) _replace_ this torn, (used) _misused_ book.
3. Are you (able) _unable_ to (pay) _repay_ the money?
4. I was (sure) _unsure_ whether she would (view) _review_ the chapter before our test.

86

Spelling: Prefixes

Directions: Using the prefixes **un**, **re** and **mis**, make new words by adding them to the given words. Use each new word in a sentence.

un mis re cover

1. cover

2. spell

3. understand

4. tie

5. write

6. adjust

7. turn

8. take

Sentences will vary.

Directions: ___ what the prefixes **dis** and **in** mean. Then add each to one of the following wo___ and write two sentences using two of the new words.

| advantage | taste | direct | secure |

87

Writing: Synonyms

A **synonym** is a word that means almost the same thing as another word.

Directions: Some words are used over and over again. Write three synonyms for each overused word below. You may want to look them up in a thesaurus, a book that lists synonyms for words.

1. good

2. nice

3. okay

4. pretty

5. little

6. big

Answers will vary.

Directions: Rewrite the paragraph below, replacing the underlined words with interesting synonyms. Add at least ten new words to the paragraph. Use your own paper if necessary.

One day in a store I saw a <u>nice</u> jacket. I wanted to buy it to replace my old jacket. I had worn my old jacket a <u>pretty</u> long time. It still looked <u>okay</u>, but I was tired of it. I didn't think my parents would buy me a new jacket, so I did something very unusual. I decided to earn some money and buy the jacket myself. My parents said that would be <u>okay</u>. I got a job cutting my neighbors' grass. When I finished, they told me I did a <u>nice</u> job. I was pretty hot and tired, but I felt <u>good</u> about making some money by myself.

Paragraphs will vary.

88

Writing: Exercising Your Imagination

Directions: Often people use the same words over and over to say that one thing is like another: as hot as fire, as cold as ice. Think of new ways to tell about things and write them below.

Example: to fly like a bird   to fly like an eagle

1. as blue as the sky

2. as soft as a cloud

3. as dark as night

4. as hard as rocks

5. as light as a feather

6. to grow like a weed

7. to swim like a fish

8. as quiet as a mouse

9. to run like the wind

10. to sleep like a baby

Answers will vary.

Now pick five of your new ways to tell about things and use them in sentences.

Answers will vary.

89

Writing: Telling What's Happening

Use a simple verb or add **ing** to tell what is happening now, using **is** or **are**.

Examples: He **talks**.   He is **talking**.
They **taste** the food.   They **are tasting** the food.

Directions: Write two sentences for each verb below. Write the verb both ways. Remember, if a verb ends with **e**, drop the **e** before adding **ing**.

Example:

rewrite

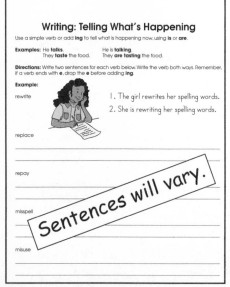

1. The girl rewrites her spelling words.
2. She is rewriting her spelling words.

replace

repay

misspell

misuse

Sentences will vary.

90

Writing: Telling What Already Happened

Add **ed** or **ing** to the verb to tell what has already happened, using **was** or **were**.

Example: She **talked**.   She **was talking**.
They **hoped**.   They **were hoping**.

Directions: Write two sentences for each verb below. Write the verb both ways.

Example:

unfasten

1. He unfastened his dog's leash.
2. He was unfastening the dog's leash.

repeat

misplace

return

ref___

remain

Sentences will vary.

91

Writing: Comparing and Contrasting

A **comparison** is a way to show the similarities and differences between two things. Another way to say this is "compare and contrast."

Directions: Practice comparing things by telling how books and movies are the same and how they are different.

1. First, make a list of the ways they are the same and a list of the ways they are different.
2. Then, use your ideas to write a paragraph about their likenesses and a paragraph about their differences. Begin both paragraphs with topic sentences. (Use more paper if needed.)
   Here is an example comparing dogs and cats.

Ways they are the same:
   both animals
   both kept as pets
   both small and furry

Ways they are different:
   cats take care of themselves
   dogs easier to teach tricks
   cats picky about their food

Topic sentences for two paragraphs:
Dogs and cats are the same in many ways.
(followed by supporting sentences giving details)

Still, no one could mistake a dog for a cat because of all the ways they are different.
(followed by supporting sentences)

Write lists comparing books and movies.

Ways they are the same:

Ways they are d___

Answers will vary.

Write two paragraphs on another sheet of paper, comparing and contrasting books and movies. Begin each paragraph with a topic sentence.

92

Writing: Comparing and Contrasting

One way to organize information for a "compare and contrast" essay is to use a Venn diagram. A **Venn diagram** is used to chart information that shows similarities and differences between two things.

Study the following example comparing apples and oranges:

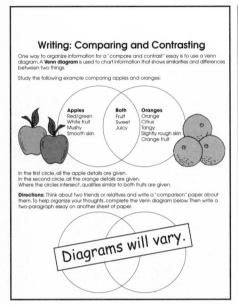

Apples
Red/green
White fruit
Mushy
Smooth skin

Both
Fruit
Sweet
Juicy

Oranges
Orange
Citrus
Tangy
Slightly rough skin
Orange fruit

In the first circle, all the apple details are given.
In the second circle, all the orange details are given.
Where the circles intersect, qualities similar to both fruits are given.

Directions: Think about two friends or relatives and write a "comparison" paper about them. To help organize your thoughts, complete the Venn diagram below. Then write a two-paragraph essay on another sheet of paper.

Diagrams will vary.

93

Review

Directions: Write several paragraphs that describe your bedroom.

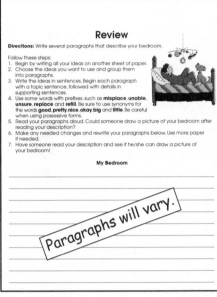

Follow these steps:
1. Begin by writing all your ideas on another sheet of paper.
2. Choose the ideas you want to use and group them into paragraphs.
3. Write the ideas in sentences. Begin each paragraph with a topic sentence, followed with details in supporting sentences.
4. Use some words with prefixes, such as **misplace, unable, unsure, replace** and **refill.** Be sure to use synonyms for the words **good, pretty, nice, okay, big** and **little.** Be careful when using possessive forms.
5. Read your paragraphs aloud. Could someone draw a picture of your bedroom after reading your description?
6. Make any needed changes and rewrite your paragraphs below. Use more paper if needed.
7. Have someone read your description and see if he/she can draw a picture of your bedroom!

My Bedroom

Paragraphs will vary.

94

Spelling: Suffixes

A **suffix** is a syllable added to the end of a word that changes its meaning. Here are some suffixes: **ful** as in **beautiful, ment** as in **excitement** and **ion** as in **vacation.**

Often suffixes change the way a word is used. For example, a suffix can change a noun (**beauty**) to an adjective (**beautiful**) or a verb (**excite**) to a noun (**excitement**).

Directions: Add the suffixes to make new words:

protect	+ ion	=	protection
improve	+ ment	=	improvement
cheer	+ ful	=	cheerful
disappoint	+ ment	=	disappointment
collect	+ ion	=	collection
thank	+ ful	=	thankful
invent	+ ion	=	invention
help	+ ful	=	helpful
play	+ ful	=	playful
state	+ ment	=	statement

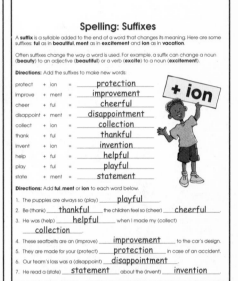

+ ion

Directions: Add **ful, ment** or **ion** to each word below.

1. The puppies are always so (play) __playful__
2. Be (thank) __thankful__ the children feel so (cheer) __cheerful__
3. He was (help) __helpful__ when I made my (collect) __collection__
4. These seatbelts are an (improve) __improvement__ to the car's design.
5. They are made for your (protect) __protection__ in case of an accident.
6. Our team's loss was a (disappoint) __disappointment__.
7. He read a (state) __statement__ about the (invent) __invention__

95

Spelling: Suffixes

Directions: Add a suffix to each word to make a new word. Then write the new word's meaning: **ion** and **ment** mean "state of being or outcome"; **ful** means "to be full of."

			Words	Meaning
rebell	+ ion	=	rebellion	the outcome of rebelling
doubt	+ ful	=	doubtful	full of doubt
pay	+ ment	=	payment	being paid
commune	+ ion	=	communion	the outcome of communing
treat	+ ment	=	treatment	being treated
beauty	+ ful	=	beautiful	full of beauty
react	+ ion	=	reaction	the outcome of reacting
amuse	+ ment	=	amusement	being amused
thank	+ ful	=	thankful	full of thanks
select	+ ion	=	selection	the outome of selecting
manage	+ ment	=	management	being managed
help	+ ful	=	helpful	full of help

Directions: Below are words with suffixes. Underline the root word and circle the suffix. The first one has been done for you.

1. resent(ment)
2. prayer(ful)
3. object(ion)
4. pay(ment)
5. sorrow(ful)
6. invent(ion)
7. content(ment)
8. adjust(ment)
9. devot(ion)
10. cheer(ful)
11. use(ful)
12. pollut(ion)

96

Spelling: Prefixes and Suffixes

Directions: Use the prefixes and suffixes below to complete the exercises.

prefix
+
base word
+
suffix

The prefix **pre** means "before." **Prepay** means "to pay before."
The prefix **dis** means "not." **Dismount** means "not mount."
The prefix **en** means "to cause or make happen." **Entrust** means "to trust."

The suffix **able** means "able to." **Likeable** means "able to like."
The suffix **less** means "without." **Painless** means "without pain."
The suffix **ness** means "a state of being." **Happiness** means "being happy."

				Words	Meanings
1.	pre	+ game	=	pregame	before game
2.	enjoy	+ able	=	enjoyable	able to enjoy
3.	dis	+ trust	=	distrust	not trust
4.	en	+ camp	=	encamp	to make camp
5.	thought	+ less	=	thoughtless	without thought
6.	eager	+ ness	=	eagerness	being eager
7.	pre	+ arrange	=	prearrange	to arrange before
8.	dis	+ content	=	discontent	not content
9.	en	+ able	=	enable	to make able
10.	home	+ less	=	homeless	without a home
11.	lovely	+ ness	=	loveliness	being lovely
12.	laugh	+ able	=	laughable	able to laugh

Directions: Select four words from above—two with prefixes and two with suffixes. Use each one correctly in a sentence.

Sentences will vary.

97

Writing: Putting Ideas Together

Directions: Combine each pair of sentences below, using conjunctions (**and, or, but, when, after, because**) and all the other ways you have learned. **Sample answers:**

1. This improvement will save lives. This improvement will also save money.
   This improvement will save lives and money.

2. Mrs. Thompson was helpful when I had trouble with math. Mrs. Thompson is my teacher.
   Mrs. Thompson, my teacher, was helpful when I had trouble with math.

3. Mike was cheerful this morning. Penny was cheerful, too.
   Mike and Penny were cheerful this morning.

4. He started to read a statement. He did not finish it.
   He started to read a statement, but he did not finish it.

5. Our team lost. We tried to hide our disappointment.
   When our team lost, we tried to hide our disappointment.

6. We were outside looking for insects. We had to make a collection for science.
   We were outside looking for insects because we had to make a collection for science.

7. No one was hurt in the accident. We were thankful.
   We were thankful when no one was hurt in the accident.

8. Is that your own invention? Is it someone else's idea?
   Is that your own invention, or is it someone else's idea?

98

123

Page 99

Spelling: Counting Syllables

Directions: Use words from the box to answer the questions.

playful	protection	disappointment	cheerful	statement
invention	improvement	thankful	collection	helpful

1. Write each word from the box on the line that tells how many syllables it has.

Two: **playful thankful cheerful statement helpful**

Three: **invention protection improvement collection**

Four: **disappointment**

2. Write words from the box that are synonyms for the ones below. Use each word only once.

discovery:	**invention**	grateful:	**thankful**
useful:	**helpful**	a repair:	**improvement**
shelter:	**protection**	joking:	**playful**
group:	**collection**	happy:	**cheerful**
sentence:	**statement**	defeat:	**disappointment**

3. Unscramble the letters to spell words from the box.

ttoonrpcel	**protection**	lipfuay	**playful**
eeclfruh	**cheerful**	tnhkuafl	**thankful**
mmeetroipvn	**improvement**	eetttanms	**statement**
ppttnniidasmeo	**disappointment**	oollccneit	**collection**
nnnlivote	**invention**	llhufpe	**helpful**

99

Page 100

Writing: Facts and Opinions

A **fact** is information that can be proven true. An **opinion** is information that tells how someone feels or what he/she thinks about something or someone.

Directions: Write an **F** by the facts and an **O** by the opinions.

F 1. The scientist announced the invention on March 4, 1990.

O 2. This invention will save the human race.

F 3. The improvement to the building cost $300.

O 4. The building is much more comfortable now.

O 5. Bob's collection of baseball cards is the best at school.

F 6. He has 139 cards in his collection.

F 7. The police provided protection for the movie star.

O 8. Without their protection, he would have been hurt.

O 9. He looks more cheerful today than yesterday.

O 10. You should be thankful I'm your sister.

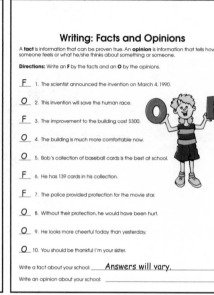

Write a fact about your school: **Answers will vary.**

Write an opinion about your school: _____

100

Page 101

Writing: Facts and Opinions

Directions: Write an **F** by the facts and an **O** by the opinions.

F 1. Jessie ate lunch at 12 noon.

O 2. Jessie thinks peanut butter is the best.

F 3. Wanda is the only girl on the football team.

O 4. I think football is a violent sport.

F 5. Seven people were injured on the football team last season.

F 6. Two of the football players weigh over 250 pounds!

O 7. No one should weigh 250 pounds!

O 8. I'm going to take that class over again.

O 9. I think I'm good at math.

F 10. According to this survey, math is the favorite subject of 25% of the students.

F 11. Miranda has two horses and three cats.

O 12. Miranda says riding horses at sunset is the only way to see a sunset.

F 13. Mr. Sims says Leroy is going to get the highest grade in the class.

O 14. He thought his grades weren't good enough.

F 15. At this school, we grade on the bell curve.

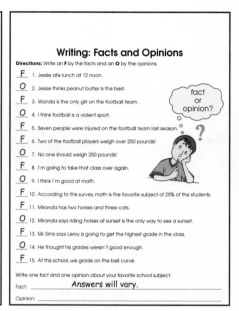

fact or opinion?

Write one fact and one opinion about your favorite school subject.

Fact: **Answers will vary.**

Opinion: _____

101

Page 102

Spelling: Finding Mistakes

Directions: Circle all the spelling mistakes in the paragraph below. (Some are from earlier lessons.) Then write each word correctly on the lines under the story.

My friendship with Justin means a lot to me. When I heard he was going to move a long distanse away, all I felt was disappointment. I just be thankful he was your friend all those years," my sister said. She was trying to be helpful but I was in pane. Justin and I got to be friends in grad one, when we shared our collections of little trucks. I remember that Justin claimed I broke his firetruck. It was an accident but he accused me of doing it on purpose. I had to replace his dumb truck! Another time, we made an invenshun. It was a new alfabet so we could write secret notes to each other. Then I misplaced our only copy. Boy, was Justin mad! I told him it was no big deal.

I'll try to look cheerful when he leaves, but I know my stomack will hurt. I'll even miss all his frekles and the way he always sneeses around my cat. At least I can call him on the fone. I might even right him a letter . . . Nah!

friendship	collections	misplaced
distance	claimed	deal
disappointment	accident	stomach
thankful	accused	freckles
helpful	replace	sneezes
pain	invention	phone
grade	alphabet	write

102

Page 103

Review

Directions: Write at least two paragraphs below. First, write facts about your favorite TV show. What is it called and when is it on? Who are some of the actors? Are they all part of one family? Where do they live? Do they have jobs?

Then write your opinions about the show. What makes it your favorite? Why do you think other people should watch it? Follow these steps:

1. Write your ideas for both paragraphs on another sheet of paper.
2. Choose the ideas you want to use. Write the facts in one paragraph and the opinions in the other. Then put the ideas in order in each paragraph and write them in sentences.
3. Try to work in some of the words with suffixes, like **cheerful, protection** and **disappointment**. Combine some of your shorter sentences with joining words.
4. Read your paragraphs aloud to see if they're clear. Make any needed changes.
5. Rewrite the paragraphs below. Use more paper if needed.
6. Give your paper to someone else. Does he/she like the same show you do?

Facts about my favorite TV show:

My opinions about

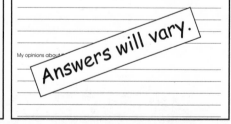

Answers will vary.

103

Page 104

Writing: All About Me

Directions: Follow the instructions to write an essay about yourself.

Think about your life so far. When were you born? When did you learn to walk, talk and run? What is your family like? Do you have any brothers or sisters or pets? Where do you live? What is your house like? What has school been like for you? Do you like school? What is your favorite grade or subject? Do you play sports? Do you have hobbies?

Use the following "cluster of ideas" chart to organize your thoughts. Number your clusters in the order they will appear in the essay. Add more clusters if needed. Write your essay on another sheet of paper, edit it using the marks on page 105 and write your final draft on page 106.

Cluster of ideas will vary.

104

Writing: Editing

Every author must edit his/her writing before making a final draft. Sometimes, even the best authors miss mistakes in their writing, and an editor will check their work much like a parent or teacher checks yours. The following editing marks are used by both editors and teachers.

Directions: Using the editing marks below, go back and edit the essay you wrote about yourself. When you have made the proper corrections, reread your essay, or have a parent or friend read it for you. Can you find any more mistakes? If so, edit your work again. When your final draft is ready, copy it on to page 106. Draw a picture to go with your essay when you are finished.

≡	capitalize letter	jenna was always late to school.
∧	insert something	Jenna was always late to school.
∧	add comma	Jenna a fourth-grade student was always late to school.
⊙	add period	Jenna was always late to school
/	make lower-case	Jenna was always late to School.
⎯	correct spelling	Jenna was awlays late to school.
∽	transpose	Jenna was late always to school.
∨ ∨	insert quotation marks	Jenna she said, "you must stop being late to school."
¶	start new paragraph	Jenna was always late to school. She tried so hard to be on time, but she couldn't manage her time. ¶ One day, as Jenna was getting ready for school, she spilled orange juice all over the front of her new shirt. She would be late again!

105

Writing: All About Me

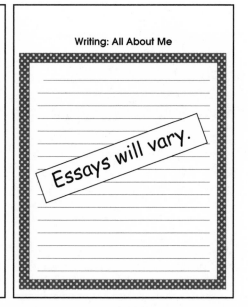

Essays will vary.

106

Teaching Suggestions

Spelling

To help your child practice phonics—letter sounds and letter patterns for sounds—obtain phonics cards or make some of your own to drill letter sound concepts. Play games with your child like "Phonics Go Fish" or "Phonics Rummy."

Ask your child to see how many new words he/she can make by simply changing the first or last letter of a word. **Example: cat, hat, sat, bat, mat, pat,** and so on.

Reinforce the "familiar" rules of spelling:
- **i** before **e** except after **c**
- Silent **e** at the end of a word changes the vowel sound to the long sound.
- When making plurals:
    Add **s**.
    If the word ends in **s, x, ch** or **sh**, add **es**.
    If the word ends in a consonant before **y**, change the **y** to **i** and add **es**.
- When making past-tense verbs:
    Add **ed**.
    If the word ends in a consonant before **y**, change the **y** to **i** and add **ed**.
    If the word ends in a vowel and a consonant, double the final consonant before adding **ed**.

Invite your child to bring home his/her weekly spelling lists from school for you to study together. Have your child:
- Write each word three times, saying the letters aloud.
- Look the words up in the dictionary, and write them in sentences, using the words correctly.
- Create a word search or crossword puzzle with the words.

Parts of Speech

Nouns — Make a noun poster with your child by dividing a large sheet of poster board into three sections and labeling them **People**, **Places** and **Things**. In each section, have your child glue magazine pictures of nouns that fit each category. For each magazine picture on the poster, invite him/her to write a corresponding proper noun.

Ask your child to name various nouns around the house; throughout your neighborhood; and on day trips to the mall, grocery story, zoo, and so on.

Verbs — To illustrate the "action" of action verbs, have your child demonstrate a given verb. **Examples: run, hop, sleep, skip, twist, smile, laugh,** and so on.

Read a short newspaper article with your child. Highlight the verbs, and ask your child to identify the verbs as action, linking or helping. You may also ask him/her to identify them as present tense, past tense or future tense.

When reading a story with your child, discuss how verbs are used to make the story more interesting and fun.

Adjectives — With your child, review the definition of adjectives as words that describe nouns. Adjectives indicate size, color, shape, texture, personality, and so on. Using your child's noun poster, have him/her think up an adjective or two for each noun shown.

Take your child to the park or out in your backyard. Invite him/her to look around, listen and smell his/her surroundings. Then ask your child to name as many adjectives as he/she can to describe the landscape, sunset, autumn leaves, wind, flowers, grass, insects, and so on.

Adverbs — With your child, review the definition of adverbs as words that describe verbs. Adverbs tell how, when or where an action takes place.

Have your child look for the use of adverbs in newspaper articles and literature. Have him/her use adverbs to describe actions going on around the house, yard, playground, library, school, and so on.

Watch a TV show or video without the sound. Have your child describe what is taking place on the screen using adjectives, nouns, adverbs and verbs.

Grammar

Review complete and incomplete sentences with your child. Discuss how a complete sentence expresses a complete thought, begins with a capital letter and ends with a punctuation mark. Review the four kinds of sentences—statement, command, question and exclamation—and the appropriate punctuation marks for each. Invite your child to look for examples of each type of sentence in newspaper articles and literature.

When writing spelling sentences, ask your child to try to write at least one of each type of sentence with the spelling words.

Write a few sentences on strips of paper. Cut the strips in two between the subject and predicate. Mix up the strips, and ask your child to put the subjects and predicates together to make complete sentences. You can also make the subject and predicate pieces fit together like puzzle pieces. When putting sentences together, your child will see how if one piece of the sentence "puzzle" is missing, the sentence is not complete.

Writing

Once your child has mastered sentence-writing skills, both informational and creative writing will become easier. As your child writes, sentence-writing skills can be taught and/or reviewed. Encourage your child to practice and experiment with all different kinds of writing—letters, poems, stories, journals, essays, informational paragraphs, book reports, TV show reviews, and so on.

Encourage your child to keep a journal. Help him/her select various topics to write about. Give your child the opportunity to write without the pressure of being "perfect." Tell him/her to write freely and express thoughts, feelings, and so on.

Maintain a "picture file" of interesting photographs from magazines and newspapers. These can often be used as a springboard for writing. Make a calendar of writing topics for each month. Topics should be appropriate for each month and season.

When your child needs to write five or six paragraphs about a given topic for school, review and help your child use the "Story Map" and "Cluster of Ideas." (see pages 59 and 70–73). If the prospect of writing a multi-paragraph story overwhelms your child, help him/her break down the assignment into smaller tasks of one or two paragraphs each. Ask your child to make sure his/her topic sentences are clear and that his/her supporting details relate to the main idea of the paragraphs.

Encourage your child to use all the steps of the writing process—brainstorming, organizing, writing, editing and final draft. When writing the first draft, your child should feel no pressure to write "perfectly," so he/she can write thoughts and ideas freely. Remind him/her that when shortcuts are taken, the writing is usually not as good as it could be.

Review the editing process with your child. Write several paragraphs that include some errors in spelling, capitalization and punctuation. Have your child edit each paragraph, using the editing marks from page 105. Did he/she find all the errors? Were the editing marks used correctly? Have your child rewrite the paragraph correctly.

Writing Topics
Following are ideas your child can use to inspire his/her writing.
1. The four seasons

Fall
Leaves changing color
Harvest
Cider
Football games
Returning to school

Winter
Colder temperatures
Snow
Bare winter trees
Sledding
Cold winter wind

Spring
Renewing of life
Spring rains

Summer
School's out
Swimming